D0378836

Praise for A Vision for **2012**

"Recommended reading for all those seeking guidance in approaching the next years of rapid transformation, frightening danger, and real potential for a planetary shift from eco-cidal corporate domination to sustainability based on collaborative communities and a new ethos of compassion."
—**Daniel Pinchbeck, author of** *2012: The Return of Quetzalcoatl*

" … [Petersen's] insights into our revolutionary age still are enlightening, and often astonishing. As the Paul Revere of the early twenty-first century, his message is this: The future is here! He is a visionary with an ethical dimension and is a too-little-known national asset. This deceptively short essay is a primer for an explosive future that is already upon us … "
—**Senator Gary Hart**

"A fascinating tour of how to think about the near future and the potential chaos and opportunities it offers. Petersen explains how, if we plan now for resilience against the plausible worst, we may come out masters of our fate rather than the opposite."
—**R. James Woolsey, former director of Central Intelligence**

"We are slip-sliding into an epochal discontinuity of culture and economy. Petersen sees clearly what it represents and offers a coherent view of our options in the face of it. He is among a very few deep thinkers doing the intellectual heavy lifting for a society otherwise lost in raptures of triviality. "
—**James Howard Kunstler, author of**
World Made By Hand **and** *The Long Emergency*

"This little book is full of provocative insights certain to help the reader respond more effectively to both the crises and opportunities that lie ahead."
—**Paul Saffo, technology forecaster**

A Vision for
2012

A Vision for
2012

Planning for Extraordinary Change

John L. Petersen

FULCRUM

GOLDEN, COLORADO

Library of Congress Cataloging-in-Publication Data

Petersen, John L., 1943-
 A vision for 2012 : planning for extraordinary change / John L.
Petersen.
   p. cm.
 Includes bibliographical references.
 ISBN-13: 978-1-55591-661-9 (hardcover) 1. Political planning--United
States. 2. Political leadership--United States. I. Title.
 JK468.P64P48 2008
 320.60973--dc22
                    2008003494

Printed in Canada by Friesens Corp.
0 9 8 7 6 5 4 3 2 1

Design by Ann W. Douden

Fulcrum Publishing
4690 Table Mountain Drive, Suite 100
Golden, Colorado 80403
www.fulcrumbooks.com

CONTENTS

ACKNOWLEDGMENTS

This book really started around 1980 when Admiral Elmo Zumwalt introduced me to one of the brightest flag officers he had mentored, Rear Admiral Bill Cockell. Bill was a very thoughtful guy who, when he became director of defense policy on the National Security Council staff, invited me to come and spend some time as his deputy. It was there that I first began to see both the inner workings of government and its shortsightedness.

Soon after that, Gary Hart let me tag along in his attempts to change the country, and I looked at government for the first time through the eyes of a politician. Hart was unique in his innate ability to cast a long view. We have wondered together since then why there aren't more political leaders who naturally see beyond the next election—even though they make decisions that last long into the future.

One public servant who clearly roamed far and wide in his thinking was Andy Marshall, the venerable director of net assessment for the Office of the Secretary of Defense who thought well of a couple of my ideas and therefore allowed me to work for and with him over most of two decades. He saw some of the big changes the country and the world are going to experience long before anyone else "in the building."

Admiral Frank Kelso, when he was selected to become the chief of naval operations, asked me down to Norfolk,

Virginia, to spend two weeks with him putting together a long-range strategy for the Navy. That was good experience, setting the stage for some of what you are about to read.

Leon Fuerth and the bright people who surround him stimulated my thinking on a number of occasions, questioning government's ability to weather the storms on our horizon. There is probably no better thinker in this area than Leon.

Dick Lamm was kind enough to introduce me to Sam Scinta, Fulcrum's publisher, for which I am very appreciative.

I wrote this book and the ideas are mine, but Anna Adeyemo from my staff at The Arlington Institute spent many hours with me thinking about it and researching the supporting information. She deserves a lot of credit. Paul Alois filled in after she left and was helped by very competent interns Nina Brooks, Nicholas Perry, and James Li.

My editor, Carolyn "Whoa. You've lost me completely!" Sobczak, reminded me in the nicest way of past high school English teachers and the difference between writing for advertising (which I used to do) and crafting something that you really want people to think about. It was a pleasure.

Suzanne Elusorr and Ken Dabkowski keep The Arlington Institute going for me. I would not be able to give myself to these kinds of musings without their commitment, loyalty, and friendship. Similarly, Mark Mayle keeps farm and home together and moving forward. His wit and dedication are unparalleled.

And for more than forty years there has been dear Diane, who gives me unending joy, and a very good time.

PREFACE

This is a book to help you make sense of the crises that are setting up on a horizon that reaches out to 2012. It is also about making organizations ready for extraordinary change.

It doesn't make any difference whether the organization most dear to you is your family, your business, your place of worship, where you learn (or teach), the government, or any another institution. The problems are basically the same. The principles are the same. The essential nature of the solutions and responses are the same.

I have specifically tried to be provocative as well as reasonable, to be honest and at the same time practically idealistic. I've tried to surface the best and most effective responses for an emerging American and planetary future that is going to be nothing short of extraordinary, while at the same time pulling no punches about what is appearing in our future.

We are entering an era that is surely going to try our souls, as we beg and scream for radically new perspectives and approaches to events and combinations of threats that humanity has never had to deal with before. At the same time, amazing, unbelievable breakthroughs in knowledge, mindsets, and capabilities will emerge just in time to be applied to the looming unpredictability that will be both strange and foreboding.

Reading this book is an exercise in systems thinking: reviewing big pieces of the puzzle from a variety of sectors and trying to think systematically about how they might interact in a plausible spectrum of possibilities. It is my hope that you emerge with a new, very broad, integrated sense of what we all might live through—and change the way you live from now on.

It will become clear that I believe we are entering one of those punctuation points in the evolution of our species that will rapidly propel us into an unimaginable new era. This new world won't work at all like what we currently find familiar. Because this shift is so fundamental and acute, the most positive option will not make sense at all from this vantage so early in the transition. In the face of almost certain uncertainty, our job is to rise to the occasion, to evolve—in our thinking, our perspectives, and in our commitment to make this transition as positive as possible. We will probably become some new kind of human at the end of it all—it is that big and important.

Although some of the rapidly approaching possibilities might encourage you to think otherwise, this book is a message of hope. There really is something extremely powerful that we can do about shaping our future, but we must get about it. Time is short.

I'll lay out the many indicators that point toward this era being a time of unprecedented change, suggest what appears to be going on, propose a mindset for engaging three alternative futures, suggest some policy proposals, and float a long view for the United States.

So hang on—we're in for the biggest ride of our lives.

CHAPTER ONE

RAPIDLY CONVERGING
GLOBAL TRENDS

You never change things by fighting the existing reality.
To change something, build a new model that makes the
existing model obsolete.

—*R. Buckminster Fuller*

The world is stepping off of a precipice into an era of extraordinary change. All around us we see anomalous, highest-ever, once-in-a-century events whispering to us that something big is coming our way. These faint signals are trying to tell us that they mean something—they are carrying an important message. Each is a harbinger, confiding more loudly than the last, "Don't concentrate on me. Look where I'm pointing."

When you gather up a handful of these indicators and stand them together, they point very clearly toward the looming likelihood of historical, epochal change—a rapid global shift unlike any our species has lived through in the past. It will be a test unlike any other for all of us, especially government.

The coming years will strain the capabilities and

emotional capacities of individuals, organizations, agencies, and administrations in ways both strange and overpowering. There are no direction-pointing precedents for what is coming; previous big, fast, world-changing shifts happened in a world that was much simpler than ours, and there is no one alive today who lived through anything like what we're anticipating. In order to survive, we must all, starting at the highest levels, not only understand what is coming, but also adapt and adjust to the new reality. The shift has to come now, not in the middle of large-scale disruptions that will consume all efforts and resources as we just try to stay alive. Preparation is only useful before the fact.

The message is getting clearer, transmitted by many sources. These sources make up an odd collection that begins deep in the heart of conventional science, works its way through business and the economy, checks in with the attitudes and unease of common people, holds a finger to the wind of ecological and climate studies, and sits down quietly to listen to indigenous wisdom. You don't have to look hard to find the message prominently embedded in religious writings, ancient philosophers' musings, and even metaphysical missives, coming from other dimensions or a collective unconscious.

After a while, it starts to add up. One after another, week after week, the messengers line up to slip through your computer, manifest themselves as friends, show up on the news and the silver screen, jump out of books, and even poke you relentlessly in the dark from the fluid world of dreams.

It's not like this is or ever has been a secret. Priests, shamans, and holy men have been talking about the coming decade for hundreds if not thousands of years—some explicitly fingering 2012 as the year to focus on. Even some traditional scholars (good ones, to be sure), logically extrapolating from the cycles that have described all of history, have reasoned that the coming years will be extraordinary. They weren't channeling anyone; they just discovered an underlying pattern that says we're in for an inevitable major upheaval that will likely shake the underpinnings of society and government as we know them.

William Strauss and Neil Howe, two researchers from the Washington, DC, area, have established themselves over the years as extraordinary observers of American and human history. Unlike most other historians, they have studied the cyclical themes in social psychology that have described the United States from the time of the pilgrims to the present. Like a physicist looking for a structural pattern that predictably repeats itself, they looked through our ancestors and events for the underlying behavioral archetypes that describe both the past and the future. Their books, *Generations: The History of America's Future* and *The Fourth Turning: What the Cycles of History Tell Us about America's Next Rendezvous with Destiny*, seem to explode with deep wisdom about the path we came in on as well as the road to our future.

Although Strauss and Howe focus specifically on the United States, the general underlying dynamics that they use to describe American behavior can surely be adapted and applied to other Western cultures as well. The words and descriptors would differ, of course, and the cyclical-time relationships might vary, but there seems to be some real truth to the notion that there are four specific generational types that keep repeating themselves, manifesting their basic worldviews through the lives of people living in a context that is becoming ever more complex and dangerous.

Their idea is simple. There are four generational types that each last two decades or so. Your grandparents had a certain outlook that was a product of the times and their upbringing. Your parents, growing up with your grandparents and their grandparents (each of whom saw the world from a quite different perspective), greatly influenced you and the way you see yourself and the world. Your children will be the latest incarnation on this influential daisy chain, reflecting your influences, those of your parents, and those of your grandparents, in that sequence.

It makes sense. Your grandparents had a really different outlook on life and themselves than that of either you or your parents. Your folks certainly saw the world differently than you do (think of the events they lived through, how social roles and expectations changed, and so forth). And so too will you pass these social "genes" on, in their unique sequential combination, to your offspring.

According to Strauss and Howe, each of the four generations exhibits a different fundamental orientation:

1. A dominant, inner-fixated IDEALIST GENERATION grows up as increasingly indulged youths after a secular crisis; comes of age inspiring a spiritual awakening; fragments into narcissistic rising adults; cultivates principle as moralist

midlifers; and emerges as visionary elders guiding the next secular crisis.

2. A recessive REACTIVE GENERATION grows up as underprotected and criticized youths during a spiritual awakening; matures into risk-taking, alienated rising adults; mellows into pragmatic midlife leaders during a secular crisis; and maintain respect (but less influence) as reclusive elders.

3. A dominant, outer-fixated CIVIC GENERATION grows up as increasingly protected youths after a spiritual awakening; comes of age overcoming a secular crisis; unites into a heroic and achieving cadre of rising adults; sustains that image while building institutions as powerful midlifers; and emerges as busy elders attacked by the next spiritual awakening.

4. A recessive ADAPTIVE GENERATION grows up as overprotected and suffocated youths during a secular crisis; matures into risk-adverse, conformist rising adults; produces indecisive midlife arbitrator-leaders during a spiritual awakening; and maintains influence (but less respect) as sensitive elders.[1]

This generational cycle plays out, in order, over the length of a lifetime, lasting eighty to one hundred years. Notice that there are alternating dominant and recessive generations: dominant parents producing recessive children; recessive parents raising dominant kids.

When you apply these underlying structural dynamics, the United States' near future begins to get very interesting. As each generation passes from a midlife period of dominance, wherein they influence and drive the society, there is a "turning"—a transition—to where their children become the shaping forces of society. There are four turnings that make up "history's seasonal rhythm of growth, maturation, entropy, and destruction":

- The *First Turning* is a *High*, an upbeat era of strengthening institutions and weakening individualism, when a new civic order implants and the old values regime decays.

- The *Second Turning* is an *Awakening*, a passionate era of spiritual upheaval, when the civic order comes under attack from a new values regime.

- The *Third Turning* is an *Unraveling*, a downcast era of strengthening individualism and weakening institutions, when the old civic order decays and the new values regime implants.

- The *Fourth Turning* is a *Crisis*, a decisive era of secular upheaval, when the values regime propels the replacement of the old civic order with a new one.[2]

We have now entered a fourth turning, a great discontinuity that ends one epoch and begins another.

Writing in 1997, Strauss and Howe describe it well:

> Around the year 2005, a sudden spark will catalyze a Crisis mood. Remnants of the old social order will disintegrate. Political and economic trust will implode. Real hardship will beset the land, with severe distress that could involve questions of class, race, nation, and empire. Yet this time of trouble will bring seeds of social rebirth. Americans will share a regret about recent mistakes—and a resolute new consensus about what to do. The very survival of the nation will feel at stake. Sometime before the year 2025, America will pass through a great gate in history, commensurate with the American Revolution, Civil War, and twin emergencies of the Great Depression and World War II.
>
> The risk of catastrophe will be very high. The nation could erupt into insurrection or civil violence, crack up geographically, or succumb to authoritarian rule. If there is a war, it is likely to be one of maximum risk and effort—in other words, a total war. Every Fourth Turning has registered an upward ratchet in the technology of destruction, and in mankind's willingness to use it. In the Civil War, the two capital cities would surely have

incinerated each other had the means been at hand. In World War II, America invented a new technology of annihilation, which the nation swiftly put to use. This time, America will enter a Fourth Turning with the means to inflict unimaginable horrors and, perhaps, will confront adversaries who possess the same.[3]

Somehow, years in advance, they seem to have hit the nail on the head. It's pretty easy to see the present and a plausible future in that description.

Strauss and Howe also characterize this time as one of great opportunity. A chance, if not a necessity, to craft a new civic order. There could be a "renaissance of civic trust, and more … America could become a society that is *good*, by today's standards, and also one that *works*."[4]

But first, we are going to have to work our way through some extraordinary change.

CHAPTER TWO

BREAKDOWNS

Everything changes. Everything ends.

William Strauss, Neil Howe, and many other thinkers and analysts suggest that the period between 2005 and 2015 will see a confluence of economic, social, cultural, ecological, technological, geopolitical, and military distress and disruption of unprecedented magnitude. These are no longer theoretical predictions. We can now clearly see the beginning of epochal change.

Consider this recent BBC headline: "Current global consumption levels could result in a large-scale ecosystem collapse by the middle of the century, environmental group WWF has warned." One that followed read, "Climate change threatens supplies of water for millions of people in poorer countries, warns a new report from the Christian development agency Tearfund."

About the same time, *The Washington Post* wrote, "Birds, bees, bats and other species that pollinate North American plant life are losing population, according to a study released yesterday by the National Research Council."

Reuters added, "Failing to fight global warming now will cost trillions of dollars by the end of the century even without counting biodiversity loss or unpredictable events like the Gulf Stream shutting down."

Author James Howard Kunstler chimed in, writing, "The Long Emergency is going to be a tremendous trauma for the human race ... We will not believe that this is happening to us, that two hundred years of modernity can be brought to its knees by a worldwide power shortage ... The survivors will have to cultivate a religion of hope, that is, a deep and comprehensive belief that humanity is worth carrying on."[1]

Then, in a landmark report compiled by Sir Nicholas Stern for the UK government, comes the admonition "The world has to act now on climate change or face devastating economic consequences."[2] He estimated that at most, humanity has ten years before the shift is unrecoverable.

What's going on here? What does this all mean? These are extraordinary statements about massive earth changes. Are they just random trends that happen to be coincidentally showing up at the same time? Or perhaps they reflect some big, historic, underlying dynamic? Maybe the world is about to experience a shift unlike anything ever seen before.

There are reasons to believe the latter could be the case. Many sources, both conventional and unconventional, suggest that we are living in a special time—that between now and 2012, the world will undergo an epochal shift to a new era. This rapid evolution will produce a world that operates in fundamentally different ways than it has in the past.

The indicators are there. Take a closer look at what is already happening.

Demographics

More people have been born on Earth in the last fifty years than in all of the preceding five thousand years. Nearly half of those alive now are under the age of 25.[3] That's the largest youth generation in history. The overwhelming majority of these young people live in the developing world, and almost a quarter are surviving on less than a dollar a day.[4] Most of them live in huge, urban ghettos without sewer systems and the service infrastructure that the rest of us take for granted. In addition to the social stability issues, these millions of people are most at risk from threats like global pandemics and would produce an overwhelming governmental and social system failure in the face of such an event. Most of them know about the quality of life in the West. Many have access to television and have been exposed to a computer or a cell phone. They are aware of their position in life. The awareness of one's relative adversity has always been a prerequisite step on the path to major social disruption.

The Beginning of the End of Oil

Regardless of the heightened awareness that our oil resources are finite, demand for oil is growing. From 2003 to 2005, it grew from 79.8 to 84.3 million barrels per day (bpd).[5]

Supply, on the other hand, appears to have peaked. Late in 2006, Kunstler wrote,

We now have nine and a half months of "rearview mirror" action to look back and see that world oil production has retreated from its all-time high of just over 85 million barrels a day (mbd) achieved in December 2005 (just as geologist Kenneth Deffeyes of Princeton had predicted). For 2006, production has remained in the 84 mbd range every month reported so far, while demand has exceeded that.[6]

We appear to have initiated the beginning of the end of the petroleum era on this planet.

We need only look at a single example, China, to glimpse the international ramifications of the end of oil. China needs oil to maintain domestic stability. If it can't supply the liquid energy to keep its transportation sector—and hence its economy—moving ahead, it risks large-scale internal disruption. When the fact that available oil has peaked starts to become generally known, a global competition for the dwindling supply will ensue. The Chinese are now involved in a comprehensive international outreach to African countries, buying up resources (not just oil) in Nigeria, Angola, Congo, Sudan. In the near future, if China is confronted with the choice between domestic instability or using violence to secure access to decreasing supplies held by another country, will that be a hard decision? Even if the Chinese economy were to slow down, the absolute economic growth is still likely to continue, especially with pressure from India.

The report *Peaking of World Oil Production: Impacts, Mitigation, and Risk Management* prepared by Science Applications International Corporation and Management Information Services, Inc., for the Department of Energy concludes that humanity is facing asymmetric risks associated with the peaking of oil. Although mitigation actions initiated prematurely may result in a poor use of resources, late initiation of mitigation may result in severe consequences including, in the opinion of some analysts, a global depression.

As Kurt Vonnegut has said, "Here's what I think the truth is: We are all addicts of fossil fuels in a state of denial, about to face cold turkey." He added, "And like so many addicts about to face cold turkey, our leaders are now committing violent crimes to get what little is left of what we're hooked on."[7]

Species Extinction

Identifying another trouble spot in our priorities, Dr. Eric Chivian, director of the Center for Health and the Global Environment at Harvard Medical School, succinctly put his finger on the paradox of our ecological values:

> Despite an avowed reverence for life, human beings continue to destroy other species at an alarming rate, rivaling the great extinctions of the geologic past. In the process, we are foreclosing the possibility of discovering the secrets they contain for the development of new

lifesaving medicines and of invaluable models for medical research, and we are beginning to disrupt the vital functioning of ecosystems on which all life depends. We may also be losing some species so uniquely sensitive to environmental degradation that they may serve as our "canaries," warning us of future threats to human health.[8]

The speed of species extinction has forced scientists to refer to the current era as the sixth extinction event, comparable to only five other events in the known history of the biosphere (That's a few billion years!).

A good example is a "new study that shows that the oceans' fish are being depleted so fast that eating seafood might be just a memory in forty years. The researchers say more is at stake than our diet, for they find the dwindling of fish stocks hurts the world economically and the ocean environmentally."[9]

According to the Millennium Ecosystem Assessment, the challenge of reversing the degradation of ecosystems while meeting increasing demands for their services could be partially met under some scenarios that have been considered, but these involve significant changes in policies, institutions, and practices that are not currently under way. In the face of the kinds of threats that we're facing, we must ask ourselves what it takes to initiate the changes of policies, institutions, and practices that is needed to assure our survival.

Climate Change

Our climate is changing. "Earth is already as warm as at any time in the last 10,000 years, and is within 1°C of being its hottest for a million years ... Another decade of business-as-usual carbon emissions will probably make it too late to prevent the ecosystems of the north from triggering runaway climate change."[10]

Feedback loops (the self-reinforcing relationships between the change in carbon dioxide [CO_2], global warming, and other factors) appear to be driving the dynamics of climate change and, once established, are the source of an exponential increase in surface warming. The summer of 2007 saw a shocking rate of melting of the Arctic ice cap—far more than even the most pessimistic expert analysts had predicted. The National Snow and Ice Data Center in Boulder, Colorado, monitored a decrease from 2.23 million square miles of ice on August 8 to 1.6 million square miles on September 16, just six weeks later. The previously recorded low in 2005 was 2.05 million square miles. Even though 2007 turned out to be one of the coldest years in recent history, the latest assessments predict that there will be no more summer ice in the Arctic Ocean by 2012. Earlier models of less than two years ago showed that significant melting would not occur before 2050. It appears we may be entering a phase in which global warming becomes a runaway train and that our only option will be planning for living in a much warmer world with serious disruptions in food supply, social stability, and the economy.

Although the majority of the world's climate scientists

believe that global warming is being driven by increases in atmospheric pollution, there are conflicting theories about what is behind the change. Some propose that ocean warming (from undersea volcanoes) is the major influence; others point to cycling in the sun's output (which may be warming other planets as well) as the culprit. Regardless, the fact is that planetwide climate change is upon us and we will have to deal with its near-term implications.

Melting ice also means thawing permafrost, which releases large amounts of methane (ten times more effective than CO_2 at producing greenhouse gases) into the atmosphere. Scientists believe that major methane releases during ancient warming trends have been responsible for mass extinction events. In the tundra of Siberia, "researchers report that permafrost has begun to melt rapidly, and, as it does, the formerly frozen methane … is escaping into the atmosphere. In some places [during the winter of 2005], the methane bubbled up so steadily that puddles of standing water couldn't freeze even in the depths of the Russian winter."[11]

"Glaciers in the Himalayas are receding faster than in any other part of the world and, if the present rate of retreat continues, they may be gone by 2035. More than 2 billion people—a third of the world's population—rely on the Himalayas for their water."[12] Environmentalist Bill McKibben has said,

> We are forced to face the fact that a century's carelessness is now melting away the world's storehouses of ice, a melting whose momentum

may be nearing the irreversible. It's as if we were stripping the spectrum of a color, or eradicating one note from every octave. There are almost no words for such a change: it's no wonder that scientists have to struggle to get across the enormity of what is happening.[13]

An increase in global temperatures can also interfere with the workings of the ocean conveyor belt and bring another ice age to Europe. The earth's ocean system is characterized by thermal inertia. This means that it adapts slowly to global cooling and warming, but once it starts to warm up or cool down, the process will extend for a long period of time. For us, it means that even if all human emissions were to stop now, thermal inertia of the ocean could sustain an increase in global temperatures.

According to conclusions of the Intergovernmental Panel on Climate Change, a scientific intergovernmental body set up by the World Meteorological Organization and the United Nations Environment Programme, there is new and stronger evidence that most of the warming observed over the last fifty years is attributable to human activities.

Our commitment to producing more greenhouse gasses continues. In the United States, there are currently "150 new coal-fired power plants on the drawing board," according to Tara Lohan. "The amount of polluting emissions they will release is staggering—between 600 million and 1.1 billion tons of CO_2 every year, for the next 50 years. And this, according to Rainforest Action Network (RAN), will basically negate every other effort currently being considered to fight climate change."[14]

The United States is not alone in its continuation of carbon emissions. "If China to grows at 8 percent for the next nine years, its economy will double in size—and its greenhouse gas emissions can be expected roughly to double as well," wrote Paul Saunders and Vaughan Turekian.[15] "China's energy intensity (energy consumed per unit of economic output) ... is still nearly seven times that of the United States, according to the World Bank. At this rate, China's growth trajectory could add the equivalent pollution of another present-day United States to the climate system in a little more than a decade."

Major Economic Disruption

During 2003–2004, concerned about possible deflation, the Federal Reserve ran the interest rates they charged banks down so low (1 percent) that mortgage lenders began offering below-prime mortgages with little or no money down. Refinancing of existing mortgages was at an all-time high. The result was a huge increase in the number of mortgages (more than five times the number of those taken out between 2002 and 2006 than in the preceding five-year period). Many, if not most of those loans (whose real interest rate was higher than prime mortgages secured in historical ways), had extra-low payments in the loan's early years with a substantial increase in payments after the "balloon" period. People whose income would never have allowed them to own a home previous to that time were buying homes ... and those least able to pay their loans began getting second mortgages on real estate that was rapidly increasing in value to generate extra income so they could make their mortgage and credit card payments. That all ended in December 2007 when banks began to write off over $100 billion of mortgage-based securities that were judged to have far less value than previously thought. Ultimately, the loss is estimated to be as high as $580 billion.

In 2005, for the first time since 1933, the savings rate in the United States became negative. This happened around the same time that personal credit card debt reached its highest level ever (the number of U.S. credit cards in the hands of consumers grew 75 percent from 1990 to 2003, while the amount that was charged increased 350 percent. Consumer credit as a percentage of personal income has never been so high (a 30 percent increase since 2000 alone), and household debt as a percentage of house assets is at a record. Independent analysis shows that credit card defaults begin about twenty-four months after a borrower has fundamentally overextended him or herself and, therefore, based on the increase in credit cards and the even higher increase in default rate, we should expect a dramatic explosion in consumer credit defaults beginning in late 2007 and growing significantly in 2008.

This overextension is now coming home to roost. The sub-prime meltdown of 2007 is just the beginning, soon to be followed by a similar unraveling of consumer credit obligations, which will reverberate as instability in banks since many banks have a great percentage of their reserves tied up in mortgage and consumer credit–based securities. If the default rate on mortgages and consumer credit increases significantly, it could very well translate into a major threat to the solvency of banks and insurance companies. Already analysts say that the real estate market in the United States is worse now than any time since the Great Depression.

According to Warren Buffett, the current financial system is highly unstable. Highly complex financial instruments called *derivatives* are time bombs and "financial weapons of mass destruction." "Derivatives generate reported earnings that are often wildly overstated and based on estimates whose inaccuracy may not be exposed for many years," writes Buffett. "Large amounts of risk ... have become concentrated in the hands of relatively few derivatives dealers ... which can trigger serious systemic problems." Derivatives can push companies onto a "spiral that can lead to a corporate meltdown."[16]

Investor George Soros pronounced the same criticisms regarding the global financial system. He believes that unless fundamental reforms are implemented, the current system will continue on a spiral of crises.[17]

The problem is multidimensional. A couple of years ago, Stephen Roach, the chief economist at investment-banking giant Morgan Stanley, predicted that the United States has no better than a 10 percent chance of avoiding economic Armageddon.[18] He was referencing systemic imbalances in our system: the United States has to import more than $3 billion in cash every day in order to finance its current account deficit with the rest of the world; twenty years ago the total debt of U.S. households was equal to half the size of the economy—today the figure is 85 percent.

In 2004, former commerce secretary Peter Peterson was writing about the same structural theme.

> We are already effectively borrowing to fund all our domestic discretionary programs. By 2020 we will be borrowing to pay for our defense programs as well, since revenues by then will cover only benefit checks and interest on the national debt. For those who want the melancholy figures, the combined cash balance of Social Security and Medicare together moves from a modest annual deficit of $25 billion in 2003 to an unthinkable annual deficit of $783 billion in 2020. According to the trustees of the Social Security and Medicare systems, the present value of the future deficits in the two programs—they are, of course, unfunded deficits—has expanded alarmingly in recent years and now stands at $74 trillion, a staggering number that far exceeds our national net worth ($43 trillion). Technically, in other words, we really are bankrupt.[19]

Former Treasury Department analysts calculated that it would take a 69 percent hike in all federal taxes or a 95 percent hike in payroll taxes to close the projected $44 trillion gap between what the baby boomers beginning to retire in 2009 expect from Social Security and Medicare and the ability of the workforce to pay. Seventy-seven million baby boomers are going to start retiring in a couple of years, causing the number of retirees in the United States to double … while the workforce that supports them will only grow by 15 percent. We could, of course, consider spending cuts. In that case, we'd have to come up with a 100-percent-plus cut across all discretionary federal spending (which is obviously impossible) or a 45 percent cut to Social Security and Medicare.[20]

I am not aware of any politicians who would be willing to support that kind of surgery.

In the meantime, Paul Volker has predicted a large crisis within about four years, and Alan Greenspan is on record agreeing that the status quo is unsustainable.

Big Potential Surprises

If these rapidly converging trends are not enough, there are a number of other potential highly disruptive global events headed our way, any one of which could quickly and dramatically shift the direction of our future. Instead of gradually growing, like trends, these wild cards—low-probability, high-impact events—occur rapidly and are of such a magnitude that they quickly overpower the ability of human social systems to effectively deal with them. When they show up, they are shocking surprises.

The most likely surprise, perhaps, is a global epidemic. We're due for one, and bird flu appears to be on the way. In October 2007, it was discovered that the H5N1 strain of the virus had mutated into a more human-unfriendly form that has now been spread throughout Africa and Europe by migrating birds. Computer estimates built around the propagation rate of previous epidemics suggest that this one, if it comes, will be much faster and more deadly than the last major outbreak in 1918, which killed 50 to 100 million people over a period of twelve months. Projections vary from 300 million to over 1 billion people dying this time. Because the planet is crisscrossed by thousands of aircraft each day, the virus, if it mutates into a more human-transmissible form, would be spread everywhere quickly and probably run the world in about six months. The United States would feel its brunt for approximately six weeks. That time would be very tough on everyone. Workshops and war games that simulate a full-blown epidemic quickly degenerate into a situation where people stop going to work, systems fail, and deaths pile up at rates that no government can cope with. It would be a very quick and deadly body blow to the world.

Another shock that certainly could be in the works is a significant increase in the deadliness of attacks by terrorists. Nuclear or biological approaches for killing large numbers of people would have an incredible physical as well as psychological effect on a country like the United States.

A third category of possible wild cards are natural events. Bigger hurricanes and tornadoes, and more of them, will probably accompany changes in the climate, and there are suggestions that earth changes like volcanic eruptions and earthquakes may be on the increase. Two well-documented possibilities in this category include the eruption of the supervolcano that lies under Yellowstone National Park and the Atlantic tsunami that is likely to result from the eruption of the La Palma volcano in the Canary Islands.

There are additional, more otherworldly potential events, like asteroids or other such heavenly bodies—or beings—showing up. Although for many people the appearance of extraterrestrials might seem far-fetched, the reaction of summarily discounting very unusual possibilities is a response that guarantees being surprised when something like that transpires.[21]

Because of the rapidly growing interdependency of the world in which we live, the effects of these kinds of events will be magnified if they happen. Large-scale disruption is a natural by-product because closely coupled events transmit social and economic implications rapidly throughout the system. Single events like bird flu would probably become catalysts, accelerating or initiating another latent disruption like a global depression.

But the breakdowns are only half the story. An extraordinary cornucopia of world-changing breakthroughs is spilling out across the planet, generating hope that we can survive these trying times.

CHAPTER THREE

BREAKTHROUGHS

*The explosive nature of exponential growth means
it may only take a quarter of a millennium to go
from sending messages on horseback to saturating
the matter and energy in our solar system with
sublimely intelligent processes.*

—*Ray Kurzweil*

Our future will not only be populated by problems. Extraordinary breakthroughs are well within our reach. Almost everywhere one looks, new capabilities and discoveries are popping up, guaranteed to change perspectives and the way we live and work. In the process, these new inventions and transformations will change who we are and, therefore, the world. Our problems are profound and unprecedented, but it may well be that, as has happened at various punctuation periods in our history, the tools, discoveries, and perspectives needed to get us through to a new era will show up just in time to show the way. Some certainly seem to be on the way, and the rate of change in science and technology offers significant hope.

The number of new inventions and discoveries are

increasing exponentially ... and that is predictable! Ray Kurzweil, inventor extraordinaire and one of the most knowledgeable futurists on the planet, thinks about technology: information technology, biotechnology, and nanotechnology. In his groundbreaking book, *The Singularity Is Near,* Kurzweil proposes, much like Strauss and Howe, that there are underlying patterns, going back to the beginning of time on this planet, that describe human innovation and development.

Regardless of which of fifteen different development/ evolution metrics one uses (technology, biology, communications, and so forth) for identifying fundamental paradigm shifts, when they are plotted on a time-based chart, it is clear that the advent of these extraordinary disruptions in history are accelerating.

Not only are the shifts showing up closer together (by a factor of about ten), but the impact of each one is increasing by an estimated eight to nine times. So, bigger and bigger things are happening faster and faster. You might think of it in much broader terms, like the principle that underpins Moore's law, which describes the doubling of computing capability every eighteen months for the last thirty years— the same extraordinary dynamic of accelerating development is taking place across a wide range of endeavors.

Kurzweil's thesis is that this trend will continue growing at ever-greater rates until the change becomes so great and fundamental that humans become different and we enter into a dramatically new era in the history of our species.

He's got the numbers to make his case. If present trends in computing continue as technology and science suggest they will, by about 2040 a single computer will be a billion times more powerful than all of the humans on the planet. Sometime around then, Kurzweil thinks we will all start working for the machines—because we can't exist without them!

It is hard to visualize, let alone predict, the effect of a rapidly increasing series of revolutionary disruptions, each one almost an order of magnitude greater than the last one (which completely disrupted and unhinged your life). Kurzweil takes a stab at explaining it:

> The paradigm shift rate (i.e., the overall rate of technical progress) is currently doubling (approximately) every decade; that is, paradigm shift times are halving every decade (and the rate of acceleration is itself growing exponentially). So, the technological progress in the twenty-first century will be equivalent to what would require (in the linear view) on the order of 200 centuries. In contrast, the twentieth century saw only about 25 years of progress (again at today's rate of progress) since we have been speeding up to current rates. *So the twenty-first century will see almost a thousand times greater technological change than its predecessor.*[1]

That translates into, say, eighty times the technological advancement of the last century taking place in the next decade, or something near that. Development like that guarantees amazing breakthroughs immediately in our future that will change the essential nature of how we live on this planet. Ponder this when you think about the positive side of the future that is stretched out in front of us to the horizon.

It is interesting to be writing these words at a time of complete dependence upon the Internet—which only became generally known about fifteen years ago—and wonder how we'll all be communicating with each other in another dozen years. It's also interesting how we, in the developed world, at least, acclimate rather easily to this change without thinking much about it. Acclimating is going to be harder in the future. The revolutions will be disruptive enough that we will have to think seriously about them and spend time wondering what is going on and where we're all going.

These breakthroughs are not isolated to any one area or sector of activity but are manifesting themselves across almost every aspect of our lives. Incredible new capabilities are showing up almost every day that will offer us solutions and alternatives to the breakdown scenarios that seem inevitable. They signal a distinct, substantive, and explosive trend of approaching discoveries and inventions that have the potential to derail some of the worst consequences of the breakdowns.

Energy

Multiple signs point not only to the beginning of the end of oil, but also to an energy revolution within the next five years that will be equal historically to the discovery of fire. It will change everything.

Energy advances are spread across all fronts. Recent announcements trumpet new photovoltaic cells with almost 50 percent efficiency in turning the sun's radiant energy into electricity (the best current ones are around 17 percent). Wind-generated power is closer to becoming as inexpensive as conventionally generated electricity. You can order about a half-dozen normal-looking cars now that get 100 miles per gallon, including sports cars and commuter vehicles. One company claims it has a battery technology that is so light and powerful that you will be able to plug your electric car into the grid and charge it in five minutes … and then drive 300 miles. Another firm announced the development of a laptop-computer battery that will last for thirty years.

Enzymes and bacteria are being used to convert biomass (plant materials and animal waste) into hydrogen and ethanol. High-density switchgrass is being touted as feedstock for ethanol, and algae ponds may be a significant source of biodiesel fuel.

Companies are sinking windmills into the ocean to harvest the energy of tidal currents: one unit will generate enough electricity for 650 homes; they have plans for farms of these units on the ocean bottom.

From here the breakthroughs become enormous.

Superconductivity, the disappearance of electrical resistance in a material (like a wire), seems to be in view. Resistance produces heat, so everything electrical now compensates for the heat it produces. The fan that you hear on your computer is only there because copper and other materials used in the machine have resistance and produce heat that needs to be removed. All motors are larger than they theoretically need to be because they have to compensate for losses. So are the wires in your walls. One of the biggest design issues associated with next-generation computer microprocessors, for example, is dealing with the heat generated by them.

If resistance could be removed, the electrical world would be overturned. Significantly less electricity would be required. All electrical components could be much smaller. No heat would mean fans and other heat-distributing mechanics would not be necessary.

As it happens, a small company north of San Francisco believes they have solved the problem of superconductivity in room-temperature materials. They've been able to do it with polymers (plastics) in limited situations and believe that they are on the verge of being able to make plastic wires that have no resistance to electricity.

Cold fusion is also breathing again. This previously maligned technology, a presumed nuclear-fusion reaction occurring near room temperature, was reported to generate more energy out of its process than was put into it. Many labs report successfully duplicating cold-fusion experiments—but not all the time. There seem to be material problems that when worked out would produce consistent results. Consistent results would mean a generator that runs itself, taking some of its output to provide the energy to keep itself going. This "extra" energy is clearly coming from some other place, likely the larger open system. The Department of Energy took another look at cold fusion in 2006 and decided that there was enough substantive success in the field to recommend that research should continue.

The underlying physics that apparently explain things like cold fusion says there is an underlying field of energy (that has now been measured) that exists everywhere in the universe. This energy, called zero-point energy (ZPE), can be thought of in the way we think of electromagnetic radio waves—they're all over. Similarly, ZPE exists everywhere in the universe and appears to be the stuff from which everything is made. It is concentrated in hard-to-fathom quantities (imagine something the size of a sugar cube having more energy than all of the known matter in the universe!) that, if effectively mined and turned into electricity or heat, would signal the beginning of a new world. Some believe that this ZPE is where the cold fusion experiments find their over-unity output.

Cold fusion and ZPE are mentioned here because, recently, two companies have claimed to have developed devices that exhibit over-unity characteristics, and they believe they are far enough along to be close to making them available to the public. Steorn, a high-tech company in Ireland, claims they have a rotating magnetic device that generates more output than what's been put in, and its success has been supposedly confirmed by a number of outside laboratories. Although they apparently do not understand why it works, the inventors plan to make the technology public sometime in early 2008.

Another company in the United Kingdom, Ecowatts, is promoting their hot-water heater, which they say puts out twice as much energy as what is used to activate the unit and will have a production prototype in early 2008. Whether either of these companies actually brings a product to market is still uncertain, but the emergence of these and other groups working on generators and batteries appears to foreshadow a likely breakthrough in energy that will have immense implications a decade from now.

Artificial General Intelligence

Artificial general intelligence (AGI) is an area of computing where applications can become smart enough to learn and are adaptable enough to be used in an unlimited number of situations. Think of a program that functions like a person: it could learn to do things on its own. Unlike the current "expert system" artificial intelligence programs that we interact with all the time (for example, the computer voice that answers the phone when you call most companies or want to make an airline reservation), AGI systems will not be built for a specific task. They'll be like a new hire that you bring in to do a particular job, any job, and they learn how to do it—at rates that far exceed human capabilities.

Peter Voss, a leader in the industry, recently used this example of what AGI might mean in the arena of health and longevity:

- Imagine a hundred thousand PhD-level researchers focusing their total efforts on life-extension and anti-aging research.

- Imagine them working 24/7, with no distraction from grant proposals, office politics, or attractive coworkers.

- Imagine the fantastic progress we would see in finding solutions for eliminating debilitating disease and reversing the deathly effects of aging.

What if this type of capability was put to work in *every* area of human endeavor that you can think of. We should be able to anticipate social behavior, understand biology and physics in new ways, invent extraordinary new tools, and eliminate world-threatening problems. Would that would be a revolution, a paradigm shift?

This kind of world, which would necessarily attend the kinds of exponential development that Kurzweil is projecting, is amazingly hard to comprehend before it exists. In fact, because we don't know what the breakthroughs will be, we have no way to accurately visualize how things will operate. But what we do know is that it is coming and that it will be bigger than anything we have seen before. It will change our lives profoundly.

How far off is this technology? Voss thinks it is "almost certainly less than 10 years ... and quite likely less than five." You may not have 'bots extending your lifetime in five years, but they may well be doing your homework. It will be a different place.

Extraordinary Knowledge Access

The revolution in computing is spawning companion revolutions in many other areas. As our basic ability to acquire knowledge accelerates, the rate of discovery and invention will also increase the rate of change in all areas of intellectual endeavor. The rapidly evolving AGI capabilities will converge in the next five years or so rather nicely with a number of incredible advances in the capability to recognize patterns (like voices, faces, and processes), the ability to simulate and model very complex systems (like ships and airplanes … and social behavior) before having to build or experience them.

The pattern-recognition advances, for example, will make it quite reasonable and efficient to talk to computers, appliances, cars, and even homes. This verbal interface, coupled with other tactile and touch-manipulation capabilities (like those on the iPhone), will allow sophisticated voice and haptic (touch) input into all manner of tools. Significant progress is also being made in the area of thought recognition, so it is not far-fetched to believe that what you think will allow you to control some of the items in your life in the near future.

These types of input will provide increasingly simple and intuitive control over the next generation of the Internet—which will rapidly start to become intelligent. Current initiatives to develop the semantic web are moving along briskly. This next generation, Web 3.0, will begin to make the Web intelligent; it will begin to relate Google returns, for example, to your personal interests and what you already know about a subject. If Google finds an individual that is related to a search subject, the semantic web will let you know things like your friends who may know the person, what organizations the individual is associated with that are also familiar to you, and where the individual's interests intersect with yours.

In the next year or two, the basic structure of the information on the Web will begin to change so that different applications (Web browser, calendar, e-mail, etc.) will be able to easily talk to each other and work together. Answers to multilevel queries—such as what is the best price on tires for my car at a place that is open this afternoon and located within fifteen miles, or what did George Bush promise during his campaign that he hasn't delivered today—will be delivered in a matter of seconds.

Maybe it will be a combination of these capabilities or perhaps something else now being developed in stealth mode by a small, wildly innovative group holed up somewhere on the other side of the world. But whatever the breakthroughs are, soon we will see the Web shift fundamentally from being a big, passive, distributed database toward becoming a global brain—a global nervous system. A tipping point will be passed and suddenly, a new reality will rapidly emerge.

All of these new capabilities allow us to invent faster, find solutions sooner, and understand things that previously seemed incomprehensible. Keeping secrets will be harder in this world—more people will share more knowledge. The breakdowns appear so threatening because we don't see any obvious solutions for them. If answers emerge, the threats will suddenly morph into big projects that needed to be tackled with approaches that make sense. That revolution is almost certainly going to happen across all areas of life.

Biotechnology

Many people believe that this will be the decade, if not the century, of biotechnology. Almost daily, amazing advances are taking place in our ability to manipulate the essential nature of plants, animals, and people. Additionally, we are fast on our way to manufacturing almost all human body parts with artificial replacements.

Every kind of domesticated animal has been cloned: horses, cows, goats, sheep, dogs, and cats. By genetically engineering the sperm and eggs of cows, scientists have significantly extended bovine lives, made them immune to certain diseases, and altered them so that their milk is best for particular kinds of cheese.

We can now water certain kinds of genetically modified tomatoes with salt water, plant other crops that require less water than they used to, grow soybeans that are impervious to selected herbicides, raise insect-protected cotton, and sow maize that resists certain weeds.

In the human arena, biotech focuses on human augmentation and molecular modification. Scientists now believe that by 2015 every human organ will be replaceable with artificial ones, except for the brain and central nervous system. Some of those replacements, like bones, joints, and eyes, will be mechanical, yielding a growing number of cyborgs—part organism, part machine. Stomachs, lungs, bladders, and other such parts will be grown outside of the human body or inside animals. We're talking human body parts here, not animal parts.

We are on the road to being able to engineer specific

characteristics into human embryos. It seems the day is coming when parents will be able to order certain features (hair color, eye color, sex) for their planned child much the same way that we order power steering and air-conditioning on a new car.

A variation on this idea is the combination of humans and animals to produce chimeras. There is already a pig in Minnesota, for example, that is living with human blood flowing in its veins. A West Coast university says it is attempting to put a human brain in a mouse (I wonder what *that* looks like?).

Some leading scientists believe that plug-in memory chips to augment brain functioning are imminent. Think about being able to run your AGI agent through the semantic web to become broadly knowledgeable about a particular subject ... and then plugging the whole process (all of the research as well as the output) into the back of your head. Not in five years, I suppose, but probably in fifteen. Remember, eighty times the technological advancement of the last century in the next decade.

Some groups claim they have already cloned humans and are secretly raising the young duplicates beyond the reach of some government individuals who want to take the children away from their parent or caretakers. So, if it hasn't happened already, it appears that humans will probably be cloned within the next half-decade. In one sense, that's not too big of a deal—we all know how to live with twins. On the other hand, it will be the first time in the recorded history of humanity that we begin to play God by engineering our offspring. One of the end points of this line of development is the ability to select what specific kinds of characteristics we might want in our children: hair and eye color, size, mental capacity, and so forth.

But we're not only interested in duplicating ourselves; clearly we'd like to live better and longer. Biotech firms believe that around 2008, more than a decade's worth of work by biotech start-ups will begin to produce fruit. Major diseases like tuberculosis, certain types of cancer, and other well-known maladies will begin to fall to the new remedies. These successes coupled with a growing emphasis on prevention, eating well, exercise, and other interventions that rejuvenate aging cells, have already begun to generate better, longer lives for many.

Recently, Craig Venter sequenced his own personal genetic code. Companies are now offering relatively inexpensive tests to individuals to identify significant portions of their own genetic makeup. Both of these events suggest that we are on the verge of making personalized medicine available that is custom-designed for you and your problem. These kinds of focused vectors of genetic renewal could have an important impact on the health and lifespan of those who can afford them.

And then there's Aubrey de Grey. This Cambridge University researcher believes that if you, the one reading this book, are about sixty years old, you may well live to be two hundred. A series of advances will show up, one after another, just in time to keep you alive until the next breakthrough. Seven basic kinds of damage, such as cell loss, nuclear mutations, and mutant mitochondria, contribute to aging, he says. We know how to deal with five of them already and should be able to solve the problems of the last two in the next year or so. Soon after those breakthroughs, pills or shots should be available that will modify the cellular degeneration rate and quickly add thirty years to the life of a sexagenarian, keeping him around until the next breakthrough.

Dr. de Grey is not alone in envisioning this trajectory toward life extension. There are other advances being made in a number of areas that are already having measurable effects on life extension. The same genetic sequence that controls aging in humans has recently been modified in mice, producing a "super mouse" that lives five times longer than its peers, has far more energy, enjoys more sex, and doesn't get fat while eating only sixty percent more calories. If that can be translated to humans, the impact would be rather extraordinary.

It is therefore not far-fetched to suggest that within the next five to ten years the outline of what it means to be a human on this planet will substantially change for a large number of people.

With these physical changes will come shifts in values and interests. If you really thought that you would be alive at age two hundred, for example, would you live differently now than you do? Would your goals change? Would you look at the degradation of our environment, climate change, and the way we resolve international problems differently if you believed you were going to have to live in the world that you are helping to produce?

It seems likely that in the same way that people now plan for future things like retirement, they would begin to plan for their futures quite differently if the life-expectancy equation were to change. Other big breakthroughs will produce similar shifts in perspective.

Production

Increases in computing capability are providing the power for an explosion of production innovations. Nanotechnology, which concentrates on the very small, is finding ways to rearrange atoms and molecules in wildly productive ways that offer extraordinary benefits. Some of these configurations promise superconductivity, very high strengths of materials at very low weights, revolutions in batteries, supereffective medicine delivery, bacteria-free surfaces, and highly efficient solar cells, among many other advances.

Scientists, for example, have created the nanotechnology equivalent of a Trojan horse, a very small molecular cage with a pharmaceutical compound captured inside it, to smuggle a powerful chemotherapeutic drug into tumor cells, thereby increasing the drug's cancer-killing activity and reducing its toxic side effects.

Another fascinating nanotechnology breakthrough will be the effective production of nanoassemblers, extremely large numbers of extremely small machines that move atoms and molecules around into predetermined patterns. This means, theoretically, that almost anything could be built from the ground up, molecule on top of molecule, using these little machines that need only a fraction of the energy that conventional manufacturing requires and produces almost no waste or pollution.

Marrying nanomaterials with ever-smaller computer processing elements promises a new generation of "smart materials" that sense the external environment (temperature, pressure, composition) and know where they are located and can communicate the present state of things at their specific place. Such materials could, for example, turn the skin of an aircraft wing into a sensory system that would telegraph immediate changes in outside wind and weather to a computer that would respond with instantaneous compensation, producing increased safety for all aboard.

These new materials will produce energy more efficiently (as in photovoltaics and batteries), reduce pollution from current manufacturing techniques, consume far fewer raw materials, generate less heat, convert waste streams into useful supplies for other manufacturing processes, and allow us to grow more food.

Society

Up to this point, we've been scrutinizing a highly abbreviated list of changes that are presently underway. But these vectors alone beg the obvious questions: Does all of this happen without changing us? Don't our outlook, our perspectives, and our values also have to shift with all of the change that is going on around us? The answer is yes. As it turns out, Ray Kurzweil's curves for technological evolution are also mirrored in some social trends.

We are becoming ever more closely connected in

increasingly interdependent ways. Our ideas now flow boundaryless around the globe. So does money, putting all of our financial futures at risk to small numbers of traders (or nonhuman computer programs) and a handful of groups who wield unusual influence on global geopolitics and economies. Our ecological and climate problems are global, not national, problems, and yet this connectivity is rapidly reconfiguring how we carry out domestic affairs (in almost every country except North Korea, perhaps). Blogs have called into question the statements and policies of the White House, and text messaging has brought down governments in the Philippines. U.S. presidential campaigns have rapidly changed directions because of blogs and websites, and some of the largest governments in the world continue to attempt to restrict communications on the Internet because of the perceived threat to government control.

We know we're connected. We know we're closely coupled to a rapidly changing world that is headed smartly in a new direction—but it's not clear where it's going. For years, survey research has shown a growing sense of unease in Americans. We don't have a good sense of what's going on, if there is any control or direction, and where it will lead. There is an expanding awareness among an international proliferation of thoughtful people that what we are experiencing is something different. This is a unique time in history; something big is in the works.

This awareness and sensitivity to change produces one of two general responses in people. For some, there is an active reaction against the uncertainty of it all and an active reversion to familiar environments that provided security in the past. Much of the movement toward fundamental and conservative religions, wherever in the world they are, can probably be traced to a need to associate with at least one aspect in one's life that promotes unchanging truth and a commitment to principles that hark back to an earlier time of stability and comfort.

Others see the change as a signal of something new, as an evolutionary thrust pointing toward the horizon, not the past. The shifting environment seems to catalyze an inner search for connection to the larger system—whether to nature, through a new sensitivity to ecological issues, or to the larger cosmos with emerging hybrids of Eastern and Western thought interlaced with metaphysics. This group is interested in developing into something new.

If history is any guide to how social shifts ultimately shake out, then the new ideas are destined to take hold rather rapidly and insert themselves firmly into the mainstream of social convention. One can see this, for example, in the acceptance of meditation and visioning (in all of their forms and names) as reasonable options for stress reduction, postoperative palliatives, and organizational-efficiency enhancement. Institutions like Harvard Medical School and major management consulting firms now see these once New-Age, airy-fairy practices as legitimate, highly effective tools for use in the home, the workplace, and medicine.

It is interesting to theorize about where this global mind change will ultimately take us. If the accelerating shifts in the areas of technology, climate, and ecology (to name only three) are any indication, then a new human being is in our near future. Out of the crucible of all of this contextual reconfiguration will emerge a radically new sense of who we are relative to each other, the natural world, and even other dimensions in the larger universe. This is not just blind speculation; the many well-shaped and early indicators across the planet are all pointing in a common direction: toward a punctuation in the evolution of the species, very much like those that have happened multiple times in our history around other kinds of organizing forces. Along with everything else, humans are going to change.

All of these breakthroughs offer a significant counterbalance to the problematic breakdowns discussed earlier, because our problems are derivatives of how we think; our sense of who we are, how reality works, why we are here, how we are connected to other people, the planet, and even the universe all inform both what is "right" to us and what options are available. When those understandings change (as they usually do throughout one's life), then we essentially become different individuals. Our reality shifts and familiar, historical values and options are replaced by new ones that better mirror our new understanding of who we are and how the new context works.

We go through this process in a smaller but similar way every time we work through to some new level of personal development: when we get a new job, get married, move, or have children, among other things.

The difference now is that the change that confronts us is global and the implications are profound. Not only is the context changing, but we are changing—partly in response to the external shifts and partly probably from sources that we don't yet fully understand. In any case, we are becoming new entities—new people. That is essentially where our hope lies, for it is by changing that we generate the innovations and options that will allow us to negotiate the new world that is emerging.

We see new energy breakthroughs offsetting the old energy breakdowns. New ways of thinking and making things could ameliorate the pollution and waste problems that are contributing to climate change. Increasing connectivity and dependency around the world have the potential to affect problems related to isolation and resource inequity. These are the early outlines of a new approach to big solutions.

The solutions emerging are not yet adequate for the magnitude and complexity of the tasks at hand, but they clearly point toward additional near-future breakthroughs and resolutions that will shift our paradigm. Furthermore, when one looks at the underlying trajectories (think of Kurzweil's exponential rates of change), it then becomes quite reasonable to believe that concurrent rapid developments in communications infrastructure, knowledge discovery, and innovation coupled with changes in perspective are creating the conditions for us to find the solutions to our problems.

So, in one way or another, the solutions to our problems either exist, are just emerging, or can be presumed to be part of the discovery explosion that appears imminent. In the past, at key moments in our evolution, these kinds of new tools and perspectives emerged in our evolutionary process just when we needed to move ahead into a dramatic new era. Whether it was the advent of agriculture, writing, printing, the heliocentric world, the steam engine, or computers and the Internet, in every case the technologies, capabilities, or insights that fueled a new eruption in knowledge and development arrived in time to force us into a new age. It looks as though it could well happen again.

CHAPTER FOUR

UNDERSTANDING POSSIBILITIES

You can't imagine—truly imagine—
where we could be going. But you should try.

So, how do we deal with the new world that is fast surrounding us? Some of these issues are as big as any other single event in history and there are quite a few of them. Robert Ornstein and Paul Ehrlich say, "The world that made us is now gone, and the world we made is a new world, one that we have developed little capacity to comprehend."[1] So even though powerful new solutions appear to be emerging, at the same time the world is becoming more complicated than at any time in history. It's really a different place that will require significant adaptation.

What's Different Now? What Is Going On?

Although no one now alive has ever lived through a similar shift, the history of the planet as we know it suggests that these kinds of major upheavals have happened many times in the past. In fact, they are the fundamental evolutionary mechanism for the planet. Biological life moved abruptly from single-cellular life to multicellular life after a very long period of equilibrium. Then multicellular life was rapidly disrupted by a radical transformation that yielded vertebrates, which were followed rapidly by mammals, early humans, and then Homo sapiens.

Social evolution continued, moving hunter-gathers into villages and towns, and then finally resulting in the printing press, which fundamentally changed how information was propagated throughout the species and ultimately enabled both the scientific and industrial age. Perhaps the computer or the Internet represents the new communications infrastructure that will be interpreted as the platform for the era we are just completing.

It appears we have entered another punctuation period, moving toward a new equilibrium of human evolution. Patterns from the past suggest that the time is right for another major shift. What might that mean to the way we think and live?

If the events that are materializing are as substantial as they appear, then this shift is going to be very big and deep. All of us will need to move into a new mode of living and thinking in order to keep from hitting the rocks and going aground.

Humans don't deal well with discontinuities and rapid change. We build our perspectives and options around the past, not generally informed about potential futures. Our underlying values and judgments are all products of experiences that are quite different from the future arrayed before us. Scientists have estimated that technology and knowledge is exploding a million times faster than the rate at which our underlying social and cognitive frameworks change. That is why there are government debates over things like cloning and stem-cell research in the United States. They reflect vain attempts to make sense of cutting-edge breakthroughs through the lens of ideas, values, and concepts that are sometimes centuries old. After all, when was the last time anyone had to wrestle with the deep significance of being half-man, half-machine, or some combination of animal and human? What about living to be two hundred? And don't forget those machines that are smarter than humans.

"The same mental routines that originally signaled abrupt physical changes in the old world are now pressed into service to perceive and decide about unprecedented dangers in the new," suggest Ornstein and Ehrlich.[2]

This change seems to be driven by an inexorable movement to higher rates of complexity and interdependence that are intrinsic to the human and planetary development process. Globalization is not just an artifact of airplanes and the Internet that shortens the effective distances between all places on the earth, although it certainly is that. No, globalization and the knowledge and communications that enable it are what happen to organisms (in this case, social human ones) as they move from simpler to more complex forms.

It's a qualitatively new world we're moving into—a nonlinear environment. It is intrinsically unpredictable and it moves through evolutionary processes with fits and starts, rapidly advancing through avalanches of change that are released by reaching certain tipping points in the system. As each of these trip wires sets off a new revolution, propelling the world into a whole new space that didn't exist before, it is easy to see why Anthony Judge thinks the trigger of a tipping point may be a combination of events, a "crisis of crises."

Judge's crisis may be the result of the five "tectonic stresses" that are accumulating deep underneath the surface of today's global order mentioned by Thomas Homer-Dixon. Individually or collectively, they could constitute such a trigger:

- **Energy stress**, especially from increasing scarcity of conventional oil

- **Economic stress** from greater global economic instability and widening income gaps between rich and poor

- **Demographic stress** from differentials in population growth rates between rich and poor societies and from expansion of megacities in poor societies

- **Environmental stress** from worsening damage to land, water, forests, and fisheries

- **Climate stress** from changes in the composition of Earth's atmosphere[3]

Former national security advisor Leon Fuerth sees the above interactions, and others related to technology, including the following, turning into potential "social tsunamis" that shake the underpinnings of the present system:

- **Geopolitical Inversion.** Geoeconomic power shifts massively and permanently to Asia, breaking the link between liberal democracy and economic primacy.

- **Environmental Dislocation.** Rapid climate change breaks fundamental links between industrial civilization and nature.

- **Evolutionary Secession.** Science and technology give us control over our own evolutionary future through manipulation of genetics and by way of symbiosis with machine intelligence.

- **Networked Governance.** Complex issues challenge the ability of representative systems of government to function with even moderate effectiveness. [4]

These transitions certainly capture some of the complexity and significance of all this upheaval, but if one really tries to visualize actually experiencing eighty times the technological advance of the last century in the next ten years, words and categories like these seem relatively flat and inadequate. It is hard to imagine how we would be able to safely navigate this path with even the most idealistic forms of our present government, economy, and society.

Possible Future Paths

How we adapt in the face of all this disruption is subject to many uncertainties. Our ability to anticipate the rapidity and magnitude of the shocks will make a great deal of difference, as will our capabilities to understand the nature of the change that is taking place. The transition to a new world will certainly tax everyone, as almost every scenario includes social upheaval. In no case will everyone agree on the path ahead, and so some, harboring great fear, will have deep differences of opinion with those who are more inclined to change. Domestic violence could well be the result.

The chance for major war will increase. It is likely that China will have energy problems and will need to find additional sources of oil. Without access to enough energy to sustain its economy, China's worsening internal stresses could certainly risk overload.[5] This could turn into an international problem of the first order as governments around the world jockey to not be left out of the dwindling-energy game. A global disruption of this kind could also call into question the future of Russia, it would seem, as China perhaps looks to its west to acquire the energy they need—using any means.

A framework for understanding which outcomes might actually manifest themselves can be found by considering the three general ways in which we respond to significant disruption. The differences center on the magnitude of the shock and the amount of infrastructure left to rebuild around.

If the shock is significant but infrastructure is basic- ally untouched, then, like with 9/11, everyone initially scrambles around a bit and new initiatives are put in place after the dust settles. But, like barriers around government buildings and airport inspectors looking for manicure scissors and tubes of shampoo, they are attempts to fight the last war, using old mind-sets. Building walls along the border with Mexico to control illegal immigration is a similar example. There is no attempt to change the under- lying incentives or reframe the issue in new terms—just the use of physical barriers to obstruct movement. There is no fundamental change in behavior.

If, like the Great Depression, the crisis is much deeper and affects large numbers of people, then the experience will sear itself on the psyche of a generation, and their whole outlook and all their values and priorities will shift. They will want to never again experience an event of that kind.

In the third case, there is an undefined threshold that if exceeded by the magnitude of the disruption both in personal and infrastructural terms, results in loss of the ability to put systems and lives back together in any reasonable period of time. In the short term, individuals rapidly shift into a mode in which they're focused on defending loved ones and salvaging belongings, caring little about what is happening elsewhere. In time, rebuilding will be attempted, but with spirit and infrastructure badly damaged, it will be very slow going.

A very recent example of this type of dynamic is Hurri- cane Katrina and New Orleans, where the psychological and physical destruction lingers long after the event. In national or global terms, the loss of the Internet would be a huge blow from which it would be very hard to rebuild.

Therefore, as we look toward 2012 with all of the converging trends and potential disruptions that are in play, history suggests that after a massive catastrophe, there are three paths to three different futures.

First, some extraordinary catalytic event or series of events shakes things up so much, so fast, that upon recovery we all rapidly decide we must live quite differently. We see ourselves and how we must live together in a significantly different way—we experience a paradigm shift and rapidly embrace fundamental change.

The legitimacy of the way we used to see and do things will suddenly be called into question by astonishing events that force the consideration of an alternative framework that appears to compensate for the systemic frailties of the previous world. This new structure will necessarily entail a very different way of understanding reality, attended ultimately by new perspectives on science, ecology, economy, cosmology, governing, agriculture, and education, among the other basic intellectual structures that support human activity. It will be a very broad-based paradigm shift.

If the shock is not too great and the basic support services and infrastructure remain in place, the new world emerging out of the transition will operate in quite a different way. In the wake of a very uncomfortable experience, like being mugged for the first time, we will quickly change our minds. A new set of priorities will emerge.

- **National security will become global security.** The

common vulnerability to global issues like climate change, an energy shift, and financial disruption, at the least, will assuredly move us toward the understanding that no country can have significant interests that are at odds with most everyone else.

- **Business and government will become acutely sensitive to the environment.** The effects of global climate change will fundamentally alter the way most of life is lived in the developed world and generate a high sensitivity to those things that sustain us.

- **Electrical energy production would increasingly become decentralized.** The peaking of the oil supply will drive research and discoveries in new areas, many of which, like solar and electric vehicles, will be far more democratic and dispersed than our present energy system.

- **Some of the economic effects of globalization will end.** There will be a new appreciation of the value and dependability of local suppliers, particularly for commodities like food.

- **New forms of current systems (government, financial, social) will emerge.** The new perspectives and values that emerge from having survived hard years of disruption will translate into new institutions and processes.

- **Interconnectivity and interdependence will become common sense.** It will be clear that we, as individuals and organizations, together with nature, are connected in important if not explicable ways that must be acknowledged.

- **Resilience will become a major focus of all institutions.** Serial disruptions will generate an emphasis on ways to absorb major blows and rapidly reconstitute the ability to continue operation.

A second scenario entails a series of major global disruptions, one after another, that degrades existing institutions and systems, but almost all of the familiar systems remain in place. Times are hard, but somehow we slowly drag ourselves into the new world. There is great pain and struggling—but all attempts to deal with the problems are variations of the status quo, adaptations of the past. We do some things differently, but there is no mind shift. The institutions work the same way, and the mirrored values form the basis of the new policies and processes. The net result is a major disruption on the historical path of human progress, but nothing more. We begin to slowly rebuild again in new but not radical ways.

In the third scenario, shocks to the global social system are so great that it fails. Governments fail. Economies fail. Human life attempts to regroup with far fewer people living far simpler lives.

Thomas Homer-Dixon, author of *The Upside of Down,*

writes about Jack Goldstone, a sociologist at George Mason University and a leading authority on revolution, who has shown that societies are far more likely to break down when they're overloaded by converging stresses—say, rapid population growth, scarcity of key resources, and a financial crisis. "Massive state breakdown is likely to occur," he writes, "only when there are simultaneously high levels of distress and conflict at several levels of society."[6]

"When a society collapses," Homer-Dixon himself writes,

> it rapidly loses complexity. Its internal organization and institutions, laws, and technologies become dramatically simpler, while its inhabitants' range of social roles and potential behaviors is sharply narrowed. Many people suffer, because without complex institutions, technologies, and social roles, societies can't keep large populations living well. After collapse, people consume far less, move around far less, communicate far less, and die far sooner.[7]

These three scenarios provide a basis for systematically thinking about what we should be doing now in anticipation of such possibilities.

Wild Cards and Black Swans

It's easy to presume that the disruptions in the above

scenarios would be natural by-products of the major break-down and breakthrough trends. That would be true, but not entirely so. There is an additional set of potential surprise events that are intrinsically either unpredictable or unlikely, which will significantly shape the coming years. The nature of these events are so profound that one of them could be the primary defining event of the era, dwarfing some of the other options that seem more likely. A climate shift that rapidly turns into an ice age (say, in a sixty-day period), would, for example, marginalize the significance of many of the other trends that we have mentioned.

Wild cards are low probability, high impact events that are so big or arrive so fast that underlying social systems cannot effectively deal with them.[8] A global bird flu pandemic is a potential wild card that would be an anticipated but unmanageable incident. Nassim Nicholas Taleb recently introduced the companion concept of "black swans": highly improbable events that are impossible to anticipate. For centuries, before the discovery of a black one in Australia, it was thought that all swans were white. No sighting of many thousands of white swans would have suggested the possibility of encountering a black swan. History offered no precedent for the future that arrived.[9]

Our survey of potential futures would be incomplete without making the provision for wild cards and black swans. Although we can't know for certain what might show up, in the context of all of this unprecedented change one can identify a number of potential paradigm-shifting events that are not on the usual planning lists of governments and corporations.[10]

- A close call with an asteroid or comet

- Global food shortage

- A rapid shift to an ice age

- Bacteria becomes immune to antibiotics

- Human cloning becomes widespread

- Civil war in China, the United States, or Russia

- Altruism breaks out

- Alternative currencies threaten national currencies

- Time travel becomes possible

- A small nation demonstrates extraordinary nanotech weapon

- China discovers major energy breakthrough

- Faster-than-light travel becomes possible

- Machines become self-aware

- Information war breaks out

- Catastrophic technological mistake threatens large numbers of people

- U.S. Federal Reserve fails

- Extraterrestrials arrive and engage us

- The return of the Awaited One

- Life discovered in other dimensions/realms

- Prediction becomes predictable

One of the common factors in these events is, of course, their size and the impact they bring. Contingency planning for the possibilities that we are already aware of (climate change and so forth) could go a good way toward preparing ourselves for those things that we don't know are coming. But, that said, some of these potential surprises do not at all lend themselves easily to advance preparations.

Options

Can we derail any of the big disruptive events that appear to be coming our way? If so, we should certainly be about it immediately. On the other hand, if offsetting the trends that are already in place is not reasonable, perhaps our time and treasure should best be spent investing in building contingency plans for dealing with the problems that we know are coming.

Both fronts demand action. First of all, a major initiative should be launched to encourage broad-based research and development in areas specifically targeted to deal with climate and energy, the most pressing issues. We should bet that the innovation trajectory we are riding will generate solutions that will allow us to shape the trends that are already in place, finding alternatives that effectively defuse some of the more painful possibilities.

Britain's Prince Charles, in a recent communication, said that "The fate of our civilization hangs in the balance" because of the inevitable implications of climate change. This is a repeating and reasonable presumption across a number of domains. Some of these big events are going to happen no matter what we try, and we should be preparing for the worst. Large-scale contingency planning should be initiated.

Research and Development

The difficulties on our horizon are so significant that all developed countries should be focusing a great deal of their attention on identifying potential solutions for them. Few things should have as much urgency.

Finding and fielding alternative energy production and climate-change mitigation capabilities should be a national priority equal to the Apollo program, which put a man on the moon. The focus should be on breakthroughs that take us to a new era beyond fossil fuels, not on investing resources in the increasingly inefficient processes of finding more oil or burning more coal. We must move *forward* rapidly.

At the same time that we push our scientists and inventors for big new ideas, we should be exploring and indentifying alternatives to the status quo in other major areas like the economy, government, ecology, and cosmology. If a new world is going to rapidly evolve, the sooner we can begin to see the shape and architecture of how it will work, the sooner we can begin to adapt.

New ethical guidelines (informed by underlying social values) that reflect the potential dangers of the arenas in which our solution-providers are working are critical.

The reason that a single person or very small groups of people can today potentially kill thousands of innocents is the historical advances that have been made in science and technology. Our tools increase our effectiveness. Future life-changing discoveries like over-unity energy and biological manipulation not only have the much-needed potential for global humanitarian solutions, but they will also offer new options for weaponization, massive mistakes, and unanticipated side effects. Everything is bigger in this new world—both the benefits and the hazards.

Contingency Planning

Every one of the scenarios we've addressed presumes major domestic disruptions within countries as well as in the continuity of global affairs. From a domestic point of view, we should, as Homer-Dixon suggests, "recognize that episodes of crisis or breakdown are not always bad things —if they're not too severe, and if societies are ready, they can create both the motivation and opportunity for renewal and regeneration."[11] This, perhaps, is the central tenet of our first future scenario, where the shock produces significant positive results.

At the same time, it is critical to understand that what we are confronting here is a *really big deal*. This is not like anything else any of us has ever experienced. There is the distinct potential that if we don't do the right thing, we'll lose everything. In two of the three alternative paths, very large numbers of people die. There will be great pain and disruption—for everyone.

Because this is a very unusual situation, an appropriate commitment cannot be too big or too soon, whether by governments, businesses, or individuals. Internationally, there are actions that ought to be taken:

- International agreements and conventions that substantially address the most pressing issues should be negotiated immediately. There should be significant incentives for everyone who actively participates and painful penalties for those who don't.

- Some agreement about sharing planetary problem-solving technology must be negotiated, incorporating a sliding-scale provision of some sort that equitably addresses the lesser-developed world.

- A high-level, multilateral initiative that considers global life under alternative scenarios should be established. Think of it as an emergency, Law of the

Sea–type process that brings all parties together to seriously consider the issues of the global commons and how all involved might function together in different fundamental contexts.

It is an understatement to mention that initiatives of these types will not succeed without extraordinary leadership. In the end, this will take bigger-than-life commitments by statesmen, the likes of which neither the United States nor the rest of the world has produced in generations. A commitment must be made to put in place bold, well-funded, and strongly supported proposals to prepare the country to anticipate what might be on the way, encourage broad-based innovation, build new adaptability into institutions, and learn what we can from past times of great change.

In the short term, local leaders must take up the slack, beginning smaller programs that can ultimately become part of a global effort. Whether local or national, there are four general functions that must become an integral part of any organization, business, or government in order to brave the coming storm: anticipation, innovation, adaptation, and education.

Anticipation

- **We must learn how to anticipate** what is coming our way before it shows up, otherwise every big event is a surprise. This will require a commitment to **generating new future-scanning functions** (particularly within government), starting at the highest levels, encouraging theoretical work in the area of anticipatory analysis, and providing incentives for the development of new technologies.

- **Anticipatory roles and capabilities must be encouraged throughout the social system**: at the state government level, in businesses, schools, and homes and families.

- **A communications and response capability** will have to be implemented to quickly and effectively communicate early warning signals to all levels of society.

Innovation

- The rapid development of **new theories of adaptation and resilience** must be encouraged. Universities and other thoughtful institutions should be encouraged to imagine new ideas about how organizations, governments, and families can organize and prepare themselves for external shocks.

- Considerable incentives should be established **to encourage practical new ideas about living well using less energy** and other resources.

Adaptation

- A priority must be established to **make all levels of society more resilient and adaptive**. In a time of high rates of change, organizational structures must have a natural ability to adjust and change to deal with the new context.

- A major initiative must be put in place to **familiarize the general populace with the potential implications** of big changes and convince them of the importance of getting ready for the times ahead.

- **Decentralization must become a national value.** The ability of the social and economic system to weather the storms on the horizon will depend on how many essentials can be acquired locally, whether it is energy, food, or other goods and services. Supplies that have to be delivered over great distances will be vulnerable to the supply-train outages that will accompany significant national and global disruption.

- **Breakdown scenarios need to be studied** so everyone can become familiar with alternative failure modes and possibilities.

Education
- Incentives should be put in place to encourage a **search for historical models of how societies adapted** (or not) to big change.

Implementing this level of institutional change is very hard and, for governments, unprecedented. A strong leader must have clear mental pictures of both the implications of staying the course and the necessity for change coupled with a pointed sense of urgency for action. There are many reasons, therefore, why our society and our government may not be able to implement initiatives of this profound magnitude. Max Bazerman and Michael Watkins talk about this problem in their book, *Predictable Surprises: The Disasters You Should Have Seen Coming, and How to Prevent Them*. The characteristics of predictable surprises they identify provide six substantial reasons why our government and our society may hesitate to address these, our most pressing problems, and do too little too late.

Characteristics of Predictable Surprises

1. Leaders knew a problem existed and that the problem would not solve itself.

2. Organizational members recognized that a problem was getting worse over time.

3. Fixing the problem would incur significant costs in the present, while the benefits of action would be delayed.

4. Addressing predictable surprises typically requires incurring a certain cost, while the reward is avoiding a cost that is uncertain but likely to be much larger. Thus, leaders know that they can expect little credit for preventing them.

5. Decision-makers, organizations, and nations often fail to prepare for predictable surprises because of the natural human tendency to maintain the status quo.

6. A small vocal minority benefits from inaction and is motivated to subvert the actions of leaders for their own private benefit. [12]

All of these rather natural responses can be replaced by appropriate action if the level of urgency is broadly embraced, the essential nature of the problem is well communicated, and people are empowered and given the incentives to generate solutions as quickly as possible. That is the responsibility of leadership, but having a policy framework that provides implementers with guidance for moving forward will be most important.

CHAPTER FIVE

A VISION FOR GETTING TO 2012

We first imagine our future.
After that, we live it.

Until now, this discussion has been largely descriptive. What is going on? What might be in our future? The much more important issue is, what are we going to do about it?

It may not be clear yet where we are going, but what is clear is how to get where we decide we want to go. The future doesn't just happen; we make it happen. It is the product of our desires, interests, perspectives, visions, and actions. What we think and what we do makes a difference. It makes the only difference.

This is not just a meaningless platitude of the kind that is offered repeatedly at graduation ceremonies. The images that we have in our minds (or not) about what we'd like to be, where we'd like to go, and what kind of world we'd like to live in directly shape what we do. Our behavior is consistent with our worldview, and therefore contributes to sustaining it.

Most people who have made their way through school, particularly college, have watched their worldview change and in a short period have seen the options available to them open up in ways they never before anticipated. They see themselves and their possibilities in a different way ... and then they choose different directions in their lives.

For me it was the Navy. "Join the Navy, see the world," they said. It was true. I saw and experienced all kinds of things in less than a handful of years that radically altered who I believed I was and where I was going for the rest of my life.

In the face of the rapidly converging trends approaching, not only do we need to persevere, we need to be on the offense: to shape and help manifest the new world that will certainly evolve, whether we take an active role in it or not. We need a vision—something to aim for. Both an explicit and an intuitive sense of where we're going is critical to this whole transition. If you don't know where you're going, as they say, any destination will do. In this context, that approach is not a good idea.

Visions are magical. They function in strange ways to guide you to achieving them. When you see the world in terms of explicit objectives, opportunities, and options, serendipitous things seem to show up to help you get to where you want to go. You don't have to understand how they work to appreciate that visions really do work. Effective business leaders know intuitively that if they haven't hung a big exciting vision in front of their employees, then the organization will wander about rather aimlessly searching for some random objective to home in on. If they are successful in crisply communicating exceptional possibilities for the company and providing the resources to fuel them, they can literally change their world. The same can be said for an individual … and for an administration.

We need to change the world—around a new vision.

It's important to keep in mind that we're talking about a *new* world. We're not trying to build a better version of what we already have. Here is the sequence:

- Big extraordinary change happens.

- Things fail. They don't work the way they use to.

- Something new emerges.

- It operates differently. It runs on different principles and values.

In this new world, humanity has figured out how to do its business in ways that do not produce the kinds of problems that caused the old, smoldering decomposition in the first place. In this world, we certainly *learn* something from the traumatic experience.

The key to getting to this new future is a vision. We need a picture of a viable global future to guide us going forward. In practical terms, this new world needs to be pretty idealistic. After all, we're really (really!) going to build a new one in a new context, which makes all kinds of things possible that certainly wouldn't work right now. That's what we should aim for. That's the contextual objective we should carry around in our minds.

A Vision

The trends and plausible big-change events discussed here appear to potentially peak around 2012 and then settle down over the following years, maybe finding a new equilibrium by 2020. If that is what happens, then the new world we have to focus on building is one that evolves between 2012 and 2020. The question is, what would we like that world to look like? What will we try to build? That will be our vision.

In building a vision of this type, it is important to fully understand the conditions from which this new world might evolve.

Let's guess that by 2012 we will have survived a global bout with bird flu (in late 2007, it appeared the virus was, for the first time, becoming transmissible to humans). A moderate pandemic has killed 500 million people worldwide over a six-month period of crisis that negatively affected almost every aspect of modern life—governments, economies, social interaction, and others.

During the same period, the change in the planet's climate has accelerated as the positive feedback loops in the climatic system kicked in. Devastating storms have become the norm, seasons don't work the way they used to, nor does traditional agriculture, generating significant food shortages and serious broad-based disruptions in regions like the United Kingdom and the rest of Europe.

Or maybe by 2012 we've experienced a major series of global disruptions related to changes in the energy sector. Driven by a decreasing supply of oil, the biggest countries in the world have aggressively tried to capture what petroleum remains. It has turned into a war (or at least a period of very serious threats) involving the United States and China, or China and Russia. A companion breakthrough in energy sources has begun to fill in some of the major cracks in the system left from the rapidly decreasing supplies of fossil fuels, but even heroic efforts and amazing innovations are unable to take up the slack fast enough to offset the crises.

We have gotten much smarter, much faster with the advent of amazing new Web-based knowledge discovery and sense-making tools (which make it easy to understand large amounts of complex information) and have learned to manipulate life in ways never before possible. Finding solutions to big problems has gotten much easier, but implementing them still takes too much time.

Our new world will have to take into consideration the underlying trends in science and technology that are driving a great deal of change, address the biggest pressing problems that confront us, reflect changes in our values and perspectives of how we see ourselves as humans, and suggest a new social framework that describes how we will work and live together.

That new world might look like this:

Values and Perspectives
In our world of 2012, there is a new realization that we are directly related to the planet, all other people, and the rest of nature in very concrete and practical ways. It has also become clear that we are interdependent in ways that are obvious but not yet fully understood. This mind-set is reflected in …

An increased emphasis on connectedness and inter-dependence. The Internet, the global economy, the environment, and many other aspects of life have made transparent that we are all directly and indirectly connected to each other and the larger context in which we live in ways that were previously not obvious. All transactions now take these linkages into consideration. Because of this interdependence, it is logical that nonconstructive relationships are intrinsically destructive and that there has been ...

A shift toward cooperation and away from competition. The interdependencies that we live with coupled with the highly destructive potential of advanced technologies have made it obvious that finding ways of working together is much better than fighting over differences. This has translated into a ...

Commitment to conflict resolution without resorting to violence. The potential destructive capability of new technologies juxtaposed with the need to build a new world has mandated that violence, especially between developed nations, as in all-out world wars, is no longer feasible. Sophisticated methods of negotiation and influence become the main tools of persuasion.

A commitment to justice for all people. Since in an interconnected society injustice to some ultimately affects all others, a broad-based commitment to justice for all is imperative.

A world of abundance. The resolution of energy problems and the advent of advanced information-technology applications presents the possibility of a world without intrinsic scarcity. Equitable access to and distribution of food, knowledge, shelter, and work could well become possible.

Individual self-realization. The crucible of phenomenal global change would produce a new perspective of oneself and the untapped potential in each of us. A dedication to self-realization would be reflected in all aspects of human activity.

Individuals choose for themselves rather than taking their cues externally. Interdependency coupled with unsurpassed knowledge and a common allegiance to justice weakens the requirement for centralized authority.

Harmony with nature. The fact that everything that lives on this planet is connected with everything else means that we live *with* nature, actively cocreating the context within which we live. We therefore see ourselves as part of the larger, global system. Maintaining harmony with nature is a priority that produces personal, spiritual, physical, and economic benefits.

A shift toward localization. The failure of global supply chains initiates a reliance on local suppliers rather than distant ones. This is especially true with food items, for which local farmers and ranchers become preferred.

A commitment to healthy food. Fresh, healthy food is a necessity for sustaining the physical and mental requirements of living in the new world.

These values and perspectives are reflected and reinforced in all other areas:

Science and Technology
A clean, all-electric world is achieved. We have entered the post-petroleum age and the world is moving toward all-electric status. Electricity is produced by pollution-free sources that in most cases require no extracted fuel, like generators that run off tidal currents, turbines driven by deep-well-produced steam, and advanced solar and wind devices.

The global brain is rapidly evolving. Unprecedented knowledge generation, discovery, and problem resolution are everyday occurrences, spurred by exponential developments in computing and communication technologies. Intractable problems are solved with capabilities that were impossible to imagine just ten years earlier.

New agricultural methods that do not rely on synthetic petroleum-based fertilizers have become dominant. Seawater-based agriculture is becoming commonplace, encouraging food production in vast areas that previously had no freshwater for irrigation.

Pressing Problems

The challenge of environmental sustainability is resolved. Problem-solving knowledge technology and a new perspective on our relationship with nature results in significantly new ways of maintaining our environment.

We have moved beyond the petroleum age. Clean, sustainable, independent sources of energy are the only approaches that are supported.

Energy production is decentralized and more distributed. Energy production is increasingly localized, whether in vehicles or individual buildings that translate solar energy and other sources into electricity. All sources contribute to the grid, fewer central power plants are required.

Social Systems

An equitable way to have a global yet local civilization is worked out. Tensions have been balanced between the forces of globalization, universal connectivity, and inter-dependence, as well as the increasing marginalization of people and cultures that always seemed to attend those trends.

Decentralization along with an ecology of cultures is effected. Local, cultural character still colors societies, but at the same time all groups have learned how to relate effectively to the larger world.

Global issues become global interests. A communications process is in place that allows all cultures to share a current interest in pressing global issues. The world thinks and acts together for the common good.

Global security is discovered, removing the legitimacy of war. The experience of having lived through or narrowly sidestepped a major world war with unheard-of new weapons convinces the world that modern combat is not an option. Sophisticated behavior-modification approaches and incentives are developed that do not include violence.

The possibility of nuclear war is prevented with 100 percent reliability. War is not an option and nuclear war must never happen. The world community bands together to assure that nuclear weapons are eliminated or so closely constrained that the chance of their being used approaches zero.

This vision might not be as far-out as you would guess. *The Earth Charter* (see Appendix I) closely resembles this vision. It was written with the input of five thousand people, has been endorsed by numerous governments, organizations, and a multitude of individuals, and draws more than one hundred thousand people to its website each month.

Effectively transitioning to this new world will require envisioning it into reality. We will all need to use a model like the one above to build a coherent idea of what the new world might look like—the principles, values, structures, behavior—and begin to carry that common picture in our minds. We need to get together at regular times with as many others as possible to project the new images, talk about them, and debate them. We should do it as though our lives depend on it, as they probably do.

There will need to be a constant orientation of openness; we will need to have a wide aperture for seeing subtle indicators of approaching change and be receptive to newly emerging techniques of dealing with the rapidly changing world. Being close-minded to the suggestions and ideas of others will court failure, as no one individual or organization will have the capability to deal with these changes by themselves. New ideas and explanations about how reality works, at all levels, will begin to bubble up in many places; they must be openly considered and honestly evaluated. There must also be an openness to adaptation—to rapidly change when it is required.

CHAPTER SIX

A STRATEGY FOR 2012

Anyone can visualize a future.
Not many know how to get there.

What we are likely to be confronted with in the next few years will require a drastic refocusing of our priorities and a world war–like sense of urgency. If we don't rise very rapidly to the occasion, we risk very painful alternatives. We must go for broke.

For a government or corporation confronted with this rapidly filling basket of issues, there is no alternative other than a full-blown commitment to shaping and driving major change. Anyone who has worked in government is well aware of the political and bureaucratic roadblocks that are placed in the path of progress. Nevertheless, we must move past them. We need to lead into the future, not just respond to it. That must be done with both a vision and a strategy.

A clear vision gives a sense of the destination, but that is not enough. Maps, as it were, must be consulted to determine which of many possible routes is the best one to pursue (over the mountains or through the lowlands;

stopping at cities or going around them; driving part of the day, all day, or during the night) in order to arrive at the destination at the desired time and in a healthy condition. A strategy is a high-level plan of action that maps the alternative roads to the future and decides the best way to get there, taking into consideration the time and resources that are available.

The following strategy can provide a starting point for our venture into the future.

1. **The United States must clearly and unambiguously take the lead in driving this change both domestically and internationally.** No other country has the obvious capability to provide this direction and paint the global picture of hope that is required.

2. **A very clear sense of urgency must be communicated across the planet.** In words and concepts that make sense for countries, agencies, businesses, other organizations, individuals, and families, a direct message must be sent that leaves no question about the importance of the issues before us all.

3. **There must be simple clarity about objectives.** An initiative must immediately be undertaken to clearly articulate objectives that stretch the present capabilities of all parts of the system, forcing and encouraging widespread innovation.

4. **There must be a deep commitment to global cooperation.** To rise to this occasion, we must unleash the synergy that comes from agencies really working together toward a common goal and similarly encourage, in every way possible, the full participation of every country. Incentives and disincentives must be implemented that make working together the obvious choice. Existing organizational structures will need to be assessed in this light.

5. **A national innovation network must be put in place that enables a virtual environment for communications and problem solving at the highest and broadest levels.** All citizens must be viewed as potential sources of the ideas needed to go forward and must be engaged in contributing to the common problem. A system that makes it easy to offer solutions must be developed.

6. **Within both the executive and legislative branches of government, there must be an office that is responsible for "forward engagement."**[1] The heads of each would report directly to the president and the congressional leaders, respectively. All would implement horizon-scanning functions that would generate the earliest warning of impending events and develop alternative pictures of how they might play out. Alerts would be rapidly disseminated

throughout the government, informing each agency of rapidly approaching issues that need urgent attention. Each department would also have an office responsible for overview of policy proposals to assure that they contributed most effectively to the national emergency campaign.

7. **A broad-based emergent-type initiative** that allows individuals, at all levels, to contribute to solutions would greatly increase the effectiveness of this initiative. A Web-facilitated forum that collects suggestions, comments, and criticisms and compiles them in an appropriate social network that allows individuals to contribute materially (for instance, by volunteering or by finding common ways to be involved in programs and issues) as well as generate new ideas, would have the potential of activating large numbers of people around specific global change.

Policy Framework

Many different agencies will necessarily be tackling different aspects of different problems in the policy production process. Without coordination, each would develop an approach that would be unique to their agency and the interests of the particular authors. With the unusually profound and urgent nature of these issues that need to be addressed, it will be critical to ensure that all initiatives

operate together in at least addressing the common characteristics of these huge, fast-moving problems.

One approach is to identify common threads
throughout a selected list of the most pressing breakdown
issues. These seven metrics would be a good place to start:

1. **Scope**: How broad is the impact of the event?

2. **Approach/Duration:** How fast will the event
    come and how long will the effect prevail?

3. **Economics:** What will be the effect on the local
    and global economies?

4. **Geopolitics:** What will be the general effect on
    intragovernmental affairs?

5. **Psychosocial:** What level of social disruption will
    it produce?

6. **Players:** What sectors of the national and global
    system will necessarily have a stake in this event?

7. **Solutions:** What are the general characteristics of
    possible solutions?

Evaluating peak oil, rapid climate change, a financial
meltdown, and a pandemic through these lenses provides
a quick, overall sense of the key considerations for policy
development.

	Peak Oil	**Rapid Climate Change**
Scope	Global	Global
Approach/Duration of Effect	Rapid/Forever	Rapid onset/ Forever
Economics	Recession to depression	Depression
Geopolitics	Disarray	Disarray
Pyschosocial	Growing uncertainty leading to panic	Rapid panic
Players	All sectors	All sectors
Solutions	Dramatic technology breakthroughs/big changes in efficiency	Energy, technology breakthroughs/ elimination of coal/carbon sequestration/ greatly reduced emissions

Financial Collapse	Pandemic	Common Threads
Global	Global	Global
Rapid onset/5–10 years	Very rapid onset/5 years	Approach very fast/Long and deep effects
Recession to depression	If acute: depression	Severe economic disruption
Severe scrambling	Disarray	Severe disruption of international affairs
Pockets of panic/Depression	Broad-based acute defensive response	Rapid, very negative social responses
All sectors	All sectors	All sectors
Redesign major aspects of system: Social Security, deficits, derivatives, etc.	Preparation of cities and towns for dealing with situation/develop extraordinary capabilities where needed	Energy, technology breakthroughs/financial redesign, large-scale prep for shock/build resilience

Successful government attempts to deal with the combination of problems will have common threads and considerations that focus on the unusual size and implications of the underlying issues. All scenarios significantly disrupt the economy. All have unusual social psychological implications. Many are directly related to each other, requiring, for example, significant national (not just regional) emergency-response mechanisms. The White House forward engagement office would have an important role in coordinating the government responses and assuring that they are both compatible and comprehensive.

Strategic Policy Guidance

In order for each policy proposal to contribute optimally to the government-wide push, it should be consistent with a strategic policy guidance that might look like the following:

All draft policies must be specifically reviewed to assure that they ...

1.   can be implemented in the most rapid way possible.

2.   broadly consider any potential negative implications that would detract from the urgency of the national campaign.

3.   actively engage with other agencies in synergic ways to elevate individual efforts to higher levels of effectiveness.

4. are as simple as possible and compatible with environments operating at reduced efficiencies.

5. are designed to encourage the broadest involvement possible of those who are targets of the proposal.

6. promote opportunities for active bilateral and multilateral government, nongovernmental organization, and business cooperation in supporting and achieving the objective of the proposed policy.

7. provide significant incentives for innovations that help solve hard problems.

8. encourage networking, cross-fertilization, and intercommunication.

9. actively contribute to the resilience of the systems they affect.

Policy Priorities

Within each departmental area there should be a number of priorities that drive everything else. They should include:

- **The environment:** Encourage an energy breakthrough; find an effective method for carbon sequestration; rapidly reduce emissions.

- **Energy:** Encourage the development of breakthrough capabilities that will quickly move us into the new era; fund development of carbon scrubbers for coal-fired power plants and mandate immediate installation on all such facilities.

- **Science and technology:** Encourage innovation in the widest, most significant way possible; make it easy for internationals to contribute.

- **Society:** Make our citizens part of the solution; encourage and marshal participation at all levels.

- **The economy:** Appoint a commission on the twin deficits.[2] Become ruthless about dealing with the systemic problems that we face.

- **Resilience:** Make resilience central to all government activity; develop internal adaptability.

- **Anticipation:** Make anticipatory analysis an important organizational obligation of all agencies.

- **Water:** Begin a new era that seriously encourages the efficient use of water and incentivizes the development of inexpensive technologies for providing safe drinking water in all parts of the world.

- **Food:** Develop new ways of growing food that work in unusual environments and climates (like saltwater-grown plants).

- **Education:** Educate girls in the developing world; in the United States, encourage a new interest in science and mobilize the education system to be an integral contributor to the innovation that is required.

- **Enabling the younger generation:** Make a special effort to engage younger people in the discussion of the future: they are uniquely equipped to deal with the issues of this age of uncertainty.

- **Population:** Provide global incentives for population reduction, particularly in the lesser developed parts of the world.

- **Encouraging individual independence:** Nurture a sense of competency and autonomy, especially in the younger generations.

There are others, of course, but the essential idea behind each priority is that we are at a time that requires unprecedented commitment, vision, and action. We can no longer argue that we can't get something like that through the U.S. political system (or through the board of directors). Our future is at stake. We must find ways to break out of the boxes that we came here in and experience the sunlight that is outside. We must change the systems. We must change the objectives. We must encourage the people to change. We must build a new world.

CHAPTER SEVEN

A TIME OF GREAT OPPORTUNITY

If you have the ability to change the world,
you have a responsibility to do so.
If you don't, who will?

We are all blessed to live at this period of extraordinary transformation. Each in his or her own way has a special role to play in contributing to the ultimate shape and function of this new world; that is probably why we are here at this time.

Even though we have a natural tendency to focus on the negative aspects of a given situation (scientists have found that those are the things we most remember), in this case there is a far better and more appropriate response.

In fixating on the negative, we always miss or discount the positive—the other half of the equation. The future is nonlinear and therefore indeterminable. Ilya Prigogine, who won a Nobel Prize for his theories of complexity and chaos, has shown that it is impossible to predict the future with any accuracy—particularly when it comes to anything substantial. Small unanticipated events, according to the tenets of chaos theory, interact with other events in fundamentally

A Vision for **2012**   97

unpredictable ways, and out of those collisions emerge futures that had seemed implausible, if even considered.

So to presume that this is all going to turn out horribly for everyone is to make that your vision and virtually guarantee that you will be included in the group that doesn't survive well. You'll act in ways that assure it.

Alternatively, actively engaging to change the situation is the way you bias the future in your direction. Think of this as a once-in-a-lifetime opportunity to play an important and necessary role in shaping the future. After all, one could argue that people like you, people interested in a book like this one, are the vanguard of this transition. We're the ones who will set the direction; we can be the agents of change.

So, put a clear image in your mind about what you'd like your future to be and then work for it. Prigogine, writing a letter to future generations, put it quite clearly. "In my message to future generations, I would like to propose arguments designed to fight against feelings of resignation or powerlessness. The recent sciences of complexity give the lie to determinism; they insist on creativity at every level of nature. The future is not given."[1]

You and I—we can invent the future of 2012.

THE EARTH CHARTER
WWW.EARTHCHARTER.ORG

Preamble

We stand at a critical moment in Earth's history, a time when humanity must choose its future. As the world becomes increasingly interdependent and fragile, the future at once holds great peril and great promise. To move forward we must recognize that in the midst of a magnificent diversity of cultures and life forms we are one human family and one Earth community with a common destiny. We must join together to bring forth a sustainable global society founded on respect for nature, universal human rights, economic justice, and a culture of peace. Toward this end, it is imperative that we, the peoples of Earth, declare our responsibility to one another, to the greater community of life, and to future generations.

Earth, Our Home

Humanity is part of a vast, evolving universe. Earth, our home, is alive with a unique community of life. The forces of nature make existence a demanding and uncertain adventure, but Earth has provided the conditions essential to life's evolution. The resilience of the community of life and the well-being of humanity depend upon preserving a healthy biosphere with all its ecological systems, a rich variety of plants and animals, fertile soils, pure waters, and clean air. The global environment with its finite resources is a common concern of all peoples. The protection of Earth's vitality, diversity, and beauty is a sacred trust.

The Global Situation

The dominant patterns of production and consumption are causing environmental devastation, the depletion of resources, and a massive extinction of species. Communities are being undermined. The benefits of development are not shared equitably and the gap between rich and poor is widening. Injustice, poverty, ignorance, and violent conflict are widespread and the cause of great suffering. An unprecedented rise in human population has overburdened ecological and social systems. The foundations of global security are threatened. These trends are perilous—but not inevitable.

The Challenges Ahead

The choice is ours: form a global partnership to care for Earth and one another or risk the destruction of ourselves and the diversity of life. Fundamental changes are needed in our values, institutions, and ways of living. We must realize that when basic needs have been met, human development is primarily about being more, not having more. We have the knowledge and technology to provide for all and to reduce our impacts on the environment. The emergence of a global civil society is creating new opportunities to build a democratic and humane world. Our environmental, economic, political, social, and spiritual challenges are interconnected, and together we can forge inclusive solutions.

Universal Responsibility

To realize these aspirations, we must decide to live with a sense of universal responsibility, identifying ourselves with the whole Earth community as well as our local communities. We are at once citizens of different nations and of one world in which the local and global are linked. Everyone shares responsibility for the present and future well-being of the human family and the larger living world. The spirit of human solidarity and kinship with all life is strengthened when we live with reverence for the mystery of being, gratitude for the gift of life, and humility regarding the human place in nature.

We urgently need a shared vision of basic values to provide an ethical foundation for the emerging world community. Therefore, together in hope we affirm the following interdependent principles for a sustainable way of life as a common standard by which the conduct of all individuals, organizations, businesses, governments, and transnational institutions is to be guided and assessed.

Principles

I. Respect and Care for the Community of Life

1. Respect Earth and life in all its diversity.

2. Care for the community of life with understanding, compassion, and love.

3. Build democratic societies that are just, participatory, sustainable, and peaceful.

4. Secure Earth's bounty and beauty for present and future generations.

In order to fulfill these four broad commitments, it is necessary to:

II. Ecological Integrity

5. Protect and restore the integrity of Earth's ecological systems, with special concern for biological diversity and the natural processes that sustain life.

6. Prevent harm as the best method of environmental protection and, when knowledge is limited, apply a precautionary approach.

7. Adopt patterns of production, consumption, and reproduction that safeguard Earth's regenerative capacities, human rights, and

community well-being.

8. Advance the study of ecological sustainability and promote the open exchange and wide application of the knowledge acquired.

III. Social and Economic Justice

9. Eradicate poverty as an ethical, social, and environmental imperative.

10. Ensure that economic activities and institutions at all levels promote human development in an equitable and sustainable manner.

11. Affirm gender equality and equity as pre-requisites to sustainable development and ensure universal access to education, health care, and economic opportunity.

12. Uphold the right of all, without discrimination, to a natural and social environment supportive of human dignity, bodily health, and spiritual well-being, with special attention to the rights of indigenous peoples and minorities.

IV. Democracy, Nonviolence, and Peace

13. Strengthen democratic institutions at all levels, and provide transparency and accountability in governance, inclusive participation in decision making, and access to justice.

14. Integrate into formal education and lifelong learning the knowledge, values, and skills needed for a sustainable way of life.

15. Treat all living beings with respect and consideration.

16. Promote a culture of tolerance, nonviolence, and peace.

The Way Forward

As never before in history, common destiny beckons us to seek a new beginning. Such renewal is the promise of these Earth Charter principles. To fulfill this promise, we must commit ourselves to adopt and promote the values and objectives of the Charter.

This requires a change of mind and heart. It requires a new sense of global interdependence and universal responsibility. We must imaginatively develop and apply the vision of a sustainable way of life locally, nationally, regionally, and globally. Our cultural diversity is a precious heritage and different cultures will find their own distinctive ways to realize the vision. We must deepen and expand the global dialogue that generated the Earth Charter, for we have much to learn from the ongoing collaborative search for truth and wisdom.

Life often involves tensions between important values. This can mean difficult choices. However, we must find ways to harmonize diversity with unity, the exercise of freedom with the common good, short-term objectives with long-term goals. Every individual, family, organization, and community has a vital role to play. The arts, sciences, religions, educational institutions, media, businesses, nongovernmental organizations, and governments are all called to offer creative leadership. The partnership of government, civil society, and business is essential for effective governance.

In order to build a sustainable global community, the nations of the world must renew their commitment to the United Nations, fulfill their obligations under existing international agreements, and support the implementation of Earth Charter principles with an international legally binding instrument on environment and development.

Let ours be a time remembered for the awakening of a new reverence for life, the firm resolve to achieve sustainability, the quickening of the struggle for justice and peace, and the joyful celebration of life.

THE ARLINGTON INSTITUTE

Founded in 1989 by futurist John L. Petersen, The Arlington Institute (TAI) is a 501(c)3 nonprofit research institute that specializes in understanding and visualizing potential impending global futures and developing powerful tools and processes for effectively preparing for the coming change.

TAI believes that we are living in an era of extraordinary global transition, the likes of which our species has never before experienced. The exponential increase of human knowledge and the acceleration of its application in technology are propelling humanity toward a new era of amazing understanding and endeavor. At the same time, this unprecedented confluence of titanic forces necessarily guarantees rapid, major disruption and change to the status quo which, if not anticipated, will be very painful.

A Time of Immense Opportunity

We must actively cocreate the future that is upon us, essentially becoming new humans, with an evolved consciousness that allows us to see the world with fresh eyes, values, and priorities ... so that we have the basis for effectively operating in a different, more compatible way with the new reality that is emerging.

We have made it our mission at TAI to help facilitate this transition and to connect and associate with like-minded people so that we may together embrace the opportunities of this future.

Among other things, TAI develops and publishes tools for anticipating, making sense of, and influencing change through a variety of active projects:

- **FUTUREdition** Our internationally heralded newsletter, published fortnightly, which chronicles current emerging events which have significant potential for shaping the future.

- **TAI Presents** A speaker series that showcases extraordinary thinkers in a public forum on subjects of particular significance related to emerging futures.

- **Humanity's Future (HF)** An intense, two-year project designed to look out 10–15 years and develop a "strategy for the future of humanity"— a vision of what a newly evolving world might look like, how it might evolve, and how individuals might best position themselves for the extraordinary change. HF will combine the inputs of a select group of unusual thinkers with the output of a large number of internationally played games designed to invent a world based upon a new set of principles (cooperation, resilience, et al.) and evolve the alternative fundamental social support systems (economy, government, ecology, cosmology, etc.) that underpin the new reality.

- **World's Biggest Problems (WBP)** A Web portal that provides a single location for understanding the most significant global problems that appear to be en route and intractable (rapid climate change, global water problems, species depletion, energy shortages, global financial disruption).

- **WHETHEReport** Since it is well established that large numbers of average people begin to anticipate significant impending events (9/11, the tsunami, etc.) in dreams and intuitions before the advent of the event, WHETHEReport will be a Web portal that collects extraordinary intuitions and dreams from individuals around the world in multiple languages and uses advanced knowledge technology to identify common patterns within the submitted narratives that can be directly related to potential future events.

The Arlington Institute is supported by a select group of individuals, foundations, corporations and government agencies, each of which realizes, in its own terms, that humanity is facing unprecedented change in the coming years. Our supporters value the uniquely creative perspective of TAI and that we provide great value in not only making sense of the rapidly emerging world around us but also pointing the way through the forest on our horizon.

The Arlington Institute
192 Fairfax Street
Berkeley Springs, WV 25411
U.S.A.
304-258-7901
www.arlingtoninstitute.org

NOTES

Rapidly Converging Global Trends

1. William Strauss and Neil Howe, *Generations: The History of America's Future, 1584–2069* (New York: William Morrow, 1990), 74.
2. William Strauss and Neil Howe, *The Fourth Turning: What the Cycles of History Tell Us about America's Next Rendezvous with Destiny* (New York: Broadway Books, 1997), 3.
3. Ibid., 6.
4. Ibid., 7.

Breakdowns

1. James Howard Kunstler, *The Long Emergency: Surviving the Converging Catastrophes of the Twenty-First Century* (New York: Atlantic Monthly Press, 2005), 20–21.
2. BBC News, "At-A-Glance: The Stern Review," BBC News, October 30, 2006, http://news.bbc.co.uk/2/hi/business/6098362.stm.
3. United Nations Population Fund, "Fast Facts," UNFPA.org, www.unfpa.org/adolescents/facts.htm.
4. Ibid.
5. Congressional Research Service, "World Oil Demand and Its Effects on Prices," June 9, 2005, www.fas.org/sgp/crs/misc/RL32530.pdf.
6. James Howard Kunstler, "Swan Dive," *The Clusterfuck Nation Chronicle: Commentary on the Flux of Events*, October 9, 2006, www.kunstler.com/mags_diary19.html.
7. Kurt Vonnegut, "Cold Turkey," *In These Times*, May 10, 2004, www.inthesetimes.com/article/cold_turkey.
8. Eric Chivian, "Environment and Health: Species Loss and Ecosystem Disruption—the Implications for Human Health," *Canadian Medical Association Journal* (January 2001).
9. David McAlary, "Ocean Fish Populations at Risk of Collapse or Extinction within 40 Years," *Voice of America*, November 2, 2006.

10. Fred Pearce, "Climate Change: 'One Degree and We're Done For," *New Scientist*, Environment, September 27, 2006.

11. Bill McKibben, "The Coming Meltdown," *The New York Review of Books*," January 12, 2006.

12. Greenpeace International, "The Global Retreat of Glaciers," Greenpeace.org, www.greenpeace.org/international/photos -videos/slideshows/the-global-retreat-of-glaciers?page=12.

13. McKibben, *Coming Meltdown*.

14. Tara Lohan, "Big Banks Are Selling Us Out on Climate Change," AlterNet, October 6, 2007, www.alternet.org/ story/64470/.

15. Paul J. Saunders and Vaughan Turekian, "Why Climate Change Can't Be Stopped," *Foreign Policy*, September 2007.

16. Warren E. Buffett, *Berkshire Hathaway Inc. 2002 Annual Report*, 2003.

17. George Soros, *The Crisis of Global Capitalism: Open Society Endangered* (New York: PublicAffairs, 1998).

18. Brett Arends, "Economic 'Armageddon' Predicted," On State Street, *Boston Herald*, November 23, 2004.

19. Peter G. Peterson, "Hear No Deficit, See No Deficit, Speak No Deficit," *Fortune*, August 9, 2004.

20. Anna Bernasek, "The $44 Trillion Abyss," *Fortune.com*, November 24, 2003. Quote from Larry Kotlikoff, Boston University.

21. Nassim Nicholas Taleb, *The Black Swan: The Impact of the Highly Improbable* (New York: Random House, 2007). A rich analysis of the shortcomings of using history as a model for anticipating disruptive futures.

Breakthroughs

1. Ray Kurzweil, "Kurzweil's Law (aka 'The Law of Accelerating Returns')," KurzweilAI.net, January 12, 2003, www.kurzweilai .net/articles/art0610.html?printable=1 (emphasis mine).

Understanding Possibilities

1. Robert Ornstein and Paul Ehrlich, *New World New Mind* (Cambridge, MA: Malor Books, 2000), 1–10.

2. Ibid., 1–13.

3. Anthony Judge, "From ECHELON to NOLEHCE: Enabling a Strategic Conversion to a Faith-Based Global Brain," Laetusin-praesens.org, August 26, 2007, www.laetusinpraesens.org/musings/nolehce.php.

4. Notes from "Societal Tsunamis" conference and workshops, Washington, DC, 2006–2007, www.forwardengagement.org.

5. Thomas Homer-Dixon, "Prepare Today for Tomorrow's Breakdown," *Toronto Globe and Mail*, May 14, 2006. Referencing the ideas of Jack Goldstone.

6. Ibid.

7. Ibid.

8. John L. Petersen, *Out of the Blue: Wild Cards and Other Big Future Surprises* (Arlington, VA: The Arlington Institute, 1997). A systematic approach to thinking about and dealing with wild cards.

9. Taleb, *The Black Swan.*

10. Petersen, *Out of the Blue.*

11. Homer-Dixon, "Prepare Today."

12. Max H. Bazerman and Michael D. Watkins, *Predictable Surprises: The Disasters You Should Have Seen Coming, and How To Prevent Them* (Cambridge, MA: Harvard Business School Press, 2004).

A Strategy for 2012

1. Leon Fuerth, Project on Forward Engagement, Rockefeller Brothers Fund and The George Washington University, Elliott School of International Affairs, www.forwardengagement.org.

2. Peter Peterson, "Hear No Deficit, See No Deficit, Speak No Deficit," *Fortune*, August 9, 2004.

A Time of Great Opportunity

1. Ilya Prigogine, "The Die Is Not Cast," Letters to Future Generations, www.unesco.org/opi2/lettres/TextAnglais/PrigogineE.html.

BIBLIOGRAPHY

Arends, Brett. "Economic 'Armageddon' Predicted," On State Street, *Boston Herald*, November 23, 2004.

Bazerman, Max H. and Michael D. Watkins. *Predictable Surprises: The Disasters You Should Have Seen Coming, and How To Prevent Them*. Cambridge, MA: Harvard Business School Press, 2004.

BBC News. "At-A-Glance: The Stern Review." *BBC News*, October 30, 2006, http://news.bbc.co.uk/2/hi/business/6098362.stm.

Bernasek, Anna. "The $44 Trillion Abyss." *Fortune.com*, November 24, 2003.

Buffett, Warren E. *Berkshire Hathaway Inc. 2002 Annual Report*, 2003. www.berkshirehathaway.com/2002ar/2002ar.pdf.

Chivian, Eric. "Environment and Health: Species Loss and Ecosystem Disruption—the Implications for Human Health." *Canadian Medical Association Journal*, January 2001.

Congressional Research Service. "World Oil Demand and Its Effects on Prices," June 9, 2005, www.fas.org/sgp/crs/misc/RL32530.pdf.

Fuerth, Leon. Project on Forward Engagment. Rockefeller Brothers Fund and The George Washington Unviersity, Elliott School of International Affairs, www.forwardengagement.org.

———. Societal Tsunamis conference and workshops. The George Washington University, Elliott School of International Affairs. Washington, DC, 2006–7, www.forwardengagement.org.

Greenpeace International. "The Global Retreat of Glaciers."

Greenpeace.org, www.greenpeace.org/international/
photosvideos/slideshows/the-global-retreat-of
-glaciers?page=12.

Homer-Dixon, Thomas. "Prepare Today for Tomorrow's
Breakdown." *Toronto Globe and Mail*, May 14, 2006.

Judge, Anthony. "From ECHELON to NOLEHCE: Enabling
a Strategic Conversion to a Faith-Based Global Brain."
Laetusinpraesens.org, August 26, 2007. www.laetusinpraesens
.org/musings/nolehce.php.

Kunstler, James Howard. *The Long Emergency: Surviving the
Converging Catastrophes of the Twenty-First Century.* New
York: Atlantic Monthly Press, 2005.

———. "Swan Dive." *The Clusterfuck Nation Chronicle:
Commentary on the Flux of Events*, October 9, 2006, www
.kunstler.com/mags_diary19.html.

Kurzweil, Ray. "Kurzweil's Law (aka 'The Law of Accelerating
Returns')." KurzweilAI.net, January 12, 2003. www
.kurzweilai.net/articles/art0610.html?printable=1.

Lohan, Tara. "Big Banks Are Selling Us Out on Climate Change."
AlterNet, October 6, 2007, www.alternet.org/story/64470.

McAlary, David. "Ocean Fish Populations at Risk of Collapse or
Extinction within 40 Years." *Voice of America*, November 2,
2006.

McKibben, Bill. "The Coming Meltdown," *The New York Review
of Books*, January 12, 2006. www.nybooks.com/articles/18616.

Ornstein, Robert and Paul Ehrlich. *New World New Mind:
Moving Toward Conscious Evolution.* Cambridge, MA: Malor
Books, 2000.

Pearce, Fred. "Climate Change: 'One Degree and We're Done
For." *New Scientist*, Environment, September 27, 2006. http://

environment.newscientist.com/article/mg19125713.300.html.

Petersen, John L. *Out of the Blue: How to Anticipate Big Future Surprises*. Lanham, MD: Madison Books, 2000.

———. *Out of the Blue: Wild Cards and Other Big Future Surprises: How to Anticipate and Respond to Profound Change*. Arlington, VA: The Arlington Institute, 1997.

Peterson, Peter G. "Hear No Deficit, See No Deficit, Speak No Deficit." *Fortune*, August 9, 2004.

Prigogine, Ilya, "The Die is Not Cast," Letters to Future Generations, www.unesco.org/opi2/lettres/TextAnglais/ PrigogineE.html.

Saunders, Paul J. and Vaughan Turekian. "Why Climate Change Can't Be Stopped." *Foreign Policy*, September 2007. www .foreignpolicy.com/story/cms.php?story_id=3980.

Soros, George. *The Collapse of Global Capitalism: Open Society Endangered*. New York: PublicAffairs, 1998.

Strauss, William and Neil Howe. *The Fourth Turning: What the Cycles of History Tell Us About America's Next Rendezvous with Destiny*. New York: Broadway Books, 1997.

Strauss, William and Neil Howe. *Generations: The History of America's Future, 1584 to 2069*. New York: William Morrow, 1990.

Taleb, Nassim Nicholas. *The Black Swan: The Impact of the Highly Improbable*. New York: Random House, 2007.

United Nations Population Fund. "Fast Facts." UNFPA.org, www .unfpa.org/adolescents/facts.htm (accessed October 10, 2007).

Vonnegut, Kurt. "Cold Turkey." *In These Times*, May 10, 2004. www.inthesetimes.com/article/cold_turkey.

ABOUT THE AUTHOR

JOHN L. PETERSEN is the founder of The Arlington Institute, a nonprofit future-oriented research institute, and the editor and publisher of *FUTUREdition*, an e-newsletter that highlights global events and items that are early indicators of potential futures. An award-winning writer, Petersen's first book, *The Road to 2015: Profiles of the Future*, was awarded Outstanding Academic Book of 1995 by *Choice* academic review magazine and remained on The World Future Society's (WFS) best-seller list for more than a year. His subsequent book, *Out of the Blue: How to Anticipate Wild Cards and Big Future Surprises*, was also a WFS best seller.

Petersen's government and political experience include stints at the National War College, the Institute for National Security Studies, the Office of the Secretary of Defense, and the National Security Council. He was a naval flight officer in the U.S. Navy and Navy Reserve and is a decorated veteran of both the Vietnam and Persian Gulf wars. He has served in senior positions for a number of presidential political campaigns and was an elected delegate to the Democratic National Convention in 1984.

Petersen lives in the eastern panhandle of West Virginia with his wife, Diane. He can be contacted at johnp@arlington-institute.org.

More thought-provoking titles in the
SPEAKER'S CORNER SERIES

Parting Shots from My Brittle Bow
    Reflections on American Politics and Life
Eugene J. McCarthy

Power of the People
    America's New Electricity Choices
Carol Sue Tombari

Social Security and the Golden Age
    An Essay on the New American Demographic
George McGovern

A Solitary War
    A Diplomat's Chronicle of the Iraq War and Its Lessons
Heraldo Muñoz

Stop Global Warming, Second Edition
    The Solution Is You!
Laurie David

TABOR and Direct Democracy
    An Essay on the End of the Republic
Bradley J. Young

Think for Yourself!
    An Essay on Cutting through the Babble, the Bias,
    and the Hype
Steve Hindes

Two Wands, One Nation
    An Essay on Race and Community in America
Richard D. Lamm

Under the Eagle's Wing
    A National Security Strategy of the United States for 2009
Gary Hart

**For more information,
visit www.fulcrumbooks.com.**